GOD'S Now Time FOR YOUR LIFE

Once again, Chuck Pierce—with sound biblical teaching and the insightful prophetic discernment on which the Body of Christ has come to rely—gives us a book that is timely for the season in which we find ourselves. He will encourage you with practical instruction for contending for your destiny and lead you into an understanding of the bigger picture: that prophetic fulfillment in our personal lives has an impact on the corporate purposes and destiny of God for cities, regions and nations. Read this book and be encouraged and equipped! The best is yet ahead!

JANE HANSEN

PRESIDENT AND CEO
AGLOW INTERNATIONAL

There is a time to battle and a time to rest, and we must be prepared for both. In *God's* Now *Time for Your Life,* Chuck Pierce explains in very clear and simple terms how to prepare for and to receive and to walk in our "now times" from God. This is a vital word for our present generation that clearly shows the biblical path from fear and hope deferred to freedom!

Chuck uses his personal experiences to bring a hands-on understanding of such subjects as recognizing and breaking old cycles of infirmity, giving hope for the destiny of our children, and prophetic fulfillment in relation to generations and territories.

First Nations people are presently discovering their unique role in the Great Commission. This book is a wonderful tool to help them fulfill this God-ordained destiny. Chuck, thank you for your obedience. This book will make a way for many.

JONATHAN MARACLE

MOHAWK, TYENDINAGA TERRITORY
DIRECTOR, BROKEN WALLS MINISTRIES
SINGER AND SONGWRITER

Chuck Pierce is a voice in this generation that God is using powerfully around the world. With great discernment and insight, Chuck lays out the tactics of the enemy to silence the prophetic word and the strategies that we must engage in to war and break through into the prophetic fulfillment that awaits us. His message is a timely word and a call for the people of God to shake off every hindrance and lay hold of the purposes of God in this critical hour.

ROBERT STEARNS

EXECUTIVE DIRECTOR, EAGLES' WINGS

For years within the circle of great men and women of God who have been apprehended for prophetic release in the Body of Christ, there has been dialogue about the "processing" and the "processes" of God. Rarely, however, have there been within the ranks of the prophetic army voices that took the time to clearly express and show us the process.

We are indebted to Chuck Pierce and Rebecca Wagner Sytsema for their willingness to put in print a manual for understanding and embracing what I call the processes and the processings—the patterns and the cycles—of God in our lives. The path to resurrection is not a straight line; it is a cycle of endings and beginnings, with key transition points that, when understood, recognized and celebrated, enable us to trust and ultimately enjoy the process.

Chuck and Rebecca have taken a major step in assisting, supporting and endorsing the work of the Spirit in our lives at this strategic season. Take time to discover the spiritual, social and economic implications of cooperating and participating with God in the proceeding word that has been spoken over your life and that continues to unfold. Chuck and Rebecca, we are indebted to you for your continued faithfulness to release what the Spirit is saying now to the Body of Christ.

MARK J. CHIRONNA, PH.D.

MARK CHIRONNA MINISTRIES
ORLANDO, FLORIDA

GOD'S *NOW TIME* FOR YOUR LIFE

CHUCK D. PIERCE
REBECCA WAGNER SYTSEMA

Regal

From Gospel Light
Ventura, California, U.S.A.

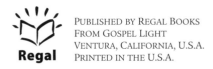

PUBLISHED BY REGAL BOOKS
FROM GOSPEL LIGHT
VENTURA, CALIFORNIA, U.S.A.
PRINTED IN THE U.S.A.

Regal Books is a ministry of Gospel Light, a Christian publisher dedicated to serving the local church. We believe God's vision for Gospel Light is to provide church leaders with biblical, user-friendly materials that will help them evangelize, disciple and minister to children, youth and families.

It is our prayer that this Regal book will help you discover biblical truth for your own life and help you meet the needs of others. May God richly bless you.

For a free catalog of resources from Regal Books/Gospel Light, please call your Christian supplier or contact us at 1-800-4-GOSPEL *or* www.regalbooks.com.

Originally published as *The Best Is Yet Ahead* by Wagner Publications in 2001.
Revised and updated edition published by Regal Books in 2005.

© 2005 Chuck Pierce and Rebecca Wagner Sytsema.
All rights reserved.

Library of Congress Cataloging-in-Publication Data
Pierce, Chuck D., 1953-
    God's now time for your life / Chuck D. Pierce, Rebecca Wagner Sytsema.
        p. cm.
    ISBN 0-8307-3834-7 (trade paper)
    1. Christian life. I. Sytsema, Rebecca Wagner. II. Title.
    BV4501.3.P54 2005
    248.4—dc22

                                                                        2005025891

1   2   3   4   5   6   7   8   9   10   /   10   09   08   07   06   05

Rights for publishing this book in other languages are contracted by Gospel Light Worldwide, the international nonprofit ministry of Gospel Light. Gospel Light Worldwide also provides publishing and technical assistance to international publishers dedicated to producing Sunday School and Vacation Bible School curricula and books in the languages of the world. For additional information, visit www.gospellightworld wide.org; write to Gospel Light Worldwide, P.O. Box 3875, Ventura, CA 93006; or send an e-mail to info@gospellightworldwide.org.

*This book is lovingly dedicated
to our children:*

*Daniel Pierce
Rebekah Pierce
John Mark Pierce
Joseph Pierce
Isaac Pierce
Ethan Pierce
Nicholas Sytsema
Samuel Sytsema
William Sytsema, III
All of our children
yet to come*

and

to all of our children's children.

*Know, dear ones; do not fear,
for the best is yet ahead!*

Contents

Introduction

When God knit you together in your mother's womb, He had a distinct purpose and timing for your life. He knew before the foundation of the world the time frame for your birth. At that point of conception, your life cycle began.

During our life cycle, we have many choices. Each day when we arise, our first thought should be, *Choose you this day whom you will serve* (see Josh. 24:15). If we serve God, we will succeed in the redemptive plan for which He created us. We will be aware of His presence. We will know when we deviate from His ultimate plan. We will also know when the enemy of our soul, Satan, attempts to interrupt that life cycle of God.

The Creator of the universe has created you and has an incredible plan for your life. Choose today whom you will serve so that your future is assured. Know this: *The best is yet ahead!*

A dear friend, Don MacAlpine, wrote this wonderful testimony:

Pilot Ejection of 1st Lt. Don MacAlpine
Mona Loa, Hawaii

It was the day before Thanksgiving, 1955, and I was the wingman of a two-plane section. We were flying FJ-2s on

a training mission and had decided to go to the big island of Hawaii and buzz the inside of Mona Loa, a volcanic crater.

As we were descending, I felt and heard an explosion from the aft end of my aircraft. I radioed my section leader and advised him. I then put out a May Day call and told them where I was and what had happened. About this time one of two red warning lights came on. (One warning light means that there is a fire in the aft end and nothing will happen until your cables burn through. The other warning light means you have approximately four seconds until the plane blows.) I couldn't tell which light was on—the whole cabin lit up red. I pulled the ejection bar and thought I had radioed my section leader that I was going out. He never heard it.

Once clear of my plane, I pulled my ripcord, which came out so easily that I thought it didn't work. My parachute opened and I thought, "All is well." My plane then crashed into the 1859 Lava Flow. Due to a full load of fuel aboard and the resulting explosion, there wasn't much left of the plane.

The whole mountainside was lava, and I landed on a flat rock. The chute snagged on a small mesquite bush. My section leader was circling overhead and I wanted to advise him that I was okay. It seemed like forever for me to stand up, retrieve a flare and set it off, but he had only circled for a quarter of a circle. I knew we were too high for a helicopter rescue, so I walked back to the crash site and spent a cold, wet night waiting for the rescue squad to arrive.

The following day the rescue squad arrived and checked the accident scene. Afterwards, I realized that I had a guardian angel looking after me. The lava rock was

so sharp that the entire rescue team had to turn in their boots for new ones. Also, that small mesquite bush was the only one in about five square miles. The wind was of a high enough velocity to have dragged me over the rocks. The sharpness of these rocks would certainly have killed me. However, that one lone bush snagged me and prevented me from being cut into shreds. Praise God! The bush became the manifestation of God in my life. Just as Moses experienced God in a bush, so did I.

At that point, even though I was not closely related to the Lord, I knew He had a plan for my life. I had seen Him in the bush. From that day forward, I have sought to follow after that plan so that my destiny could be fulfilled.

● ● ●

Just as Abraham found God's provision for the future of his generations in a bush, and just as Moses found his call (which resulted in the destiny of a nation) in a bush, so Don also met God supernaturally in a bush. Our prayer for you as you read this book is that you will be able to open your eyes and see God in the circumstances and situations around you. He is Jehovah Jireh, the One who will see to it that your destiny has been provided for and is made complete.

Blessings,
Chuck D. Pierce
Rebecca Wagner Sytsema

God's *Now* Time for Your Life

For I know the thoughts that I think toward you, says the LORD, thoughts of peace and not of evil, to give you a future and a hope.

JEREMIAH 29:11

Have you ever gotten so caught in a hard place that you wondered if you could escape? Have you ever waited so long for a promise to manifest that you lost hope? Have you known that God has given you a promise that has yet to be fulfilled? One morning I ("I" in this book refers to Chuck) awoke with the following words ringing through my spirit: *"The best is yet ahead. Do not be discouraged by what you see, for I can fulfill that which I have for your life."* I knew it was God.

THE TRUTH ABOUT THE FUTURE

Is the best yet ahead? The truth is that for the believer in Christ, the best is always ahead! We have a wonderful promise for our future—an eternal promise of communion with God. The Bible clearly tells us that we don't live down here on Earth with our sights set only on what is temporal, but that we are to have a view of eternity and operate from that perspective. God will give us grace to endure what is going on in our temporal world until we come into the fullness of our eternal destiny, which is with Him. This really is the bottom line. Even in our greatest hour here on Earth, our best is still ahead.

But is that all there is? Is our only hope for prophetic fulfillment in eternity? What about our destiny while we are still here on Earth? Yes, there is destiny to fulfill. Yes, there is more than grace to just endure our circumstances until the Lord calls us to Himself. And yes, God does have a wonderful plan for our temporal existence that will flow into our eternal communion with Him.

A TIME OF BIRTH

November 3, 1984, was a day of prophetic fulfillment for the Pierce family. It was on that autumn day in Tomball, Texas, that our beautiful daughter, Rebekah, was born. What a joyful day it was—one that followed years of anguish and waiting, believing that God would come through on His word. It was a day of prophetic fulfillment, because in 1980, God spoke to my wife, Pam, and assured her that she would have twins. At that time, however, she was barren. What an incredible promise to a woman who couldn't even conceive!

Pam's womb was filled with endometriosis—a disease that kept her body hostile to conception. The eggs were in her, but they were never able to connect in a way that would sustain life.

In other words, the potential was there, but something was blocking the eggs from being nurtured so that life could result. There is much potential in many of us to conceive and bring God's plan to fullness for our life. However, there are many issues that keep us from seeing a fulfillment of God's purpose. These are the issues that we want to address in this book.

Pam knew that for God to give her twins, He would have to heal her. She had already been waiting for six years to conceive and would wait for four more years before her healing came. But after 10 years, God kept His word and His prophetic promise to her was fulfilled.

There were many things that God had to set in order or rearrange before we saw the fruition of His promise. One of those things was our home. Before we had children our home was a beautiful show place. We could always find a comfortable chair to sit in and enjoy the quiet and the order. But, perfect as it was, our home was sterile.

For us to have children, we had to be willing to let go of our lifestyle. We had to be willing to have our perfect home messed up. We had to be willing to deal with spit-up on our carpet and the smell of dirty diapers in the air. We had to be ready for bloody noses, muddy shoes and noisy music and to have dogs, cats, birds and even snakes roaming through our home. We had to be ready for bickering and fights, for endless appointments, and for boyfriends and girlfriends. To come out of a place of barrenness and sterility, we had to be ready to receive the physical manifestation and all that it would represent in our lives, including obeying the Lord every step of the way.

LET THE HEALING BEGIN

There is a perfect time for each of us in our lives when we need to move forward into God's destiny and ultimate plan. I believe

most of us want to have God's plan for our lives, but *we* must make the choice to do what He asks us to do. In Pam's and my life, there was a series of steps that we had to go through in order to see our promise of children fulfilled.

1. The Lord required me to obey Him and encourage Pam to quit her secular job.
2. The Lord brought a wonderful child into our life that we adopted as an infant.
3. The Lord required me to leave my secular job and go into full-time ministry.
4. The Lord required us both to take positions at one of the largest children's homes in East Texas.
5. God began to extend my missions call by focusing me on the Soviet Union.
6. God had us deal with any sin, both personal and generational, that could hinder us from receiving our promise.
7. God had Pam go to our pastor and have him pray for her.
8. The Spirit of the Lord began to teach us the principle of following after God. He spoke two words to us: *"Follow Me."*
9. The Spirit of God visited me with revelation for the former Soviet Union and asked me to deliver that revelation to a key mission leader.
10. God also asked us to go to a conference that had teachings contrary to the church we were attending at the time.
11. God asked my wife to raise her hands to worship in a way that she had never worshiped before.
12. The Lord asked us to respond to His Spirit and power as it fell on us both at that conference.

As a result of following these steps of obedience, culminating at the conference when Pam, against her nature, raised her hands in worship to God, Pam was healed instantly by the power of God invading her body and actually knocking out the clots that were in her uterus. I say *instantly*, but all the steps of obedience listed above took years of discipline. After that conference, however, Pam started her first normal menstrual cycle, and as a result her womb was no longer hostile. She conceived within two weeks—and not only at that time, but four more times as well.

Obviously, these will not be the same steps of obedience that the Lord will have for everyone, but it is important to realize that there are steps of obedience that can lead anyone to prophetic fulfillment. Out of Pam's and my willingness to allow the Lord to mess up our home and disrupt our lives, He eventually gave us beautiful, wonderful children. Where there were once many places to sit and enjoy the quiet, today you can hardly find a seat in the Pierce home. But it is a home filled with love, life and promise for the future. Despite all the noise and all the commotion, we would never willingly go back to that place of sterility where our promises were locked up within us.

Prophetic fulfillment is often a messy process that can seem to interrupt the order of life. Yet even in the midst of drastic changes, there is a great joy in knowing that we are moving toward God's destiny. Our prayer for you as you read this book is that you will experience the joy of prophetic fulfillment in your own life.

STANDING ON THE PROMISES

God has a future and a hope for everyone reading this book! He has given us promises for salvation, inheritance and spiritual life. A promise is like a promissory note on which we can base our future. God has every intention of fulfilling His promises to

us. This is a statement that we can take to the bank! It is a sure foundation upon which we can confidently stand.

But how do we know God's plan for our lives? The only way is through a covenant relationship with Him. From this covenant relationship, we discover God's plan for our destiny. God has many ways of revealing His desire for our lives to us. We may get an "I know that I know" feeling within our hearts. We may encounter circumstances that we know have been directed by God that will open or close doors. We may have an urging or intense desire that God is stirring within us—something that we know we need to do in our life. We may have supernatural encounters through dreams, visions or miracles. We may be reading the Bible and see a pattern that illuminates something to us in a way that is very appropriate for our life. Or we may have a glimpse of God's destiny for us through prophetic words that we receive.

No matter what our experience has been, we all have promises from God giving us a future and a hope. He has a plan and a destiny for each of us, and He is working all things together for good to position us properly so that His plans can be fulfilled. Each time we respond to the Lord in obedience, we see progress in the overall fulfillment of our earthly purpose. This process and progression is called *prophetic fulfillment*.

GOD'S *NOW* TIME

In the natural cycle of life, there are seasons. Some seasons are filled with desolation, but in those times we can take comfort in knowing that every season has a time frame. There is a time when desolation ends and prophetic fulfillment begins. Those seasons in our lives are *now* times—times of prophetic fulfillment when God's promises are manifested.

In his tremendous book *God's Timing for Your Life*, Dutch Sheets writes:

Life is a series of changes—a process of going from the old to the new—from *chronos* [a general process of time] to *kairos* [an opportune, strategic, or *now* time]. Growth, change, revival—all are processes. Life is connected. Not understanding this, we tend to despise the *chronos* times of preparing, sowing, believing and persevering. . . . We're not losing or wasting time, we're investing it. And if we do so faithfully, the shift *will* come.[1]

That was the case in our family when 10 years of barrenness came to an end with the birth of our first child. When a time of desolation or wilderness ends and a new season of promise begins, those are God's *now* times.

In Daniel 9, we see a biblical example of a desolation season coming to an end so that a season of prophetic fulfillment could begin. Israel had been in captivity in Babylon for 70 years and was still in bondage when Daniel began reading the prophecies of Jeremiah: "In the first year of his reign I, Daniel, understood by the books the number of the years specified by the word of the LORD through Jeremiah the prophet, that He would accomplish seventy years in the desolations of Jerusalem" (v. 2). As Daniel read, he suddenly understood that there was a prophecy given many years before and that *now* was the time for the prophecy to be fulfilled. The 70 years of desolation that Jeremiah had prophesied had been completed and the time had come to break out of captivity.

God always has *now* times in our lives. Daniel knew that it was time for this word to be fulfilled and for captivity to end. We, like Daniel, also need to come to a place in which we understand God's time sequence. I know that in my own life, when it is time for a season of desolation to end, I want it done and its effects off of me. And once I get out of it, I don't want to turn back. That's the attitude we need to have in moving forward into

prophetic fulfillment. We need to be in close enough relationship with God so that we know when to start into a new sequence and a new cycle of life. We need to know when it is time to cast off our desolation and move into a new season.

BREAKING OUT OF DESOLATION

"Then I set my face toward the Lord God to make request by prayer and supplications, with fasting, sackcloth, and ashes" (v. 3). As Daniel came to an understanding that the times were changing and that Israel needed to break out of captivity, he did two things: He turned to God and dialogued with Him through prayer and supplications, and he began to deny himself through fasting so that all desolation could be broken. By doing these two things, he reconciled himself with God and, as a representative of Israel, broke out of the season of desolation. This allowed the process to begin for the Israelites to break out of captivity and move into their future.

Through His promises to us, God is breaking off desolation personally, corporately and territorially—and hell hates it. Any time that we are getting ready to break forth into a new season of prophetic fulfillment, Satan will oppose us and try to keep us in the desolation of the past. There is a three-step process for us to be aware of as we move out of desolation toward *now* times in our lives.

Step One: God Gives an Intercessory Call
As was the case with Daniel, God often first releases an intercessory burden in our lives. A burden is a deep impression of God's heart and will within our spirit. This burden feels like a weight or a stirring within us that is so strong that we must respond to God so that change can come into our lives or environment. This is how intercession begins.

Intercession always proceeds what God is doing to break desolation from our lives. Prophetic fulfillment is a continuing process. In other words, all that God has done, even in the midst of the desolation season, has a purpose and will work together to move us into what He has for us in our new place. Dutch Sheets writes:

> God wants to shift our thinking from becoming discouraged during these times to realizing the necessity of *chronos* seasons. . . . Knowing that we are cooperating with God and giving Him what He needs to bring the new, we can rejoice over, rather than despise, small beginnings.[2]

We need to get in line with what God is doing and connect ourselves with it for our now season. We need to respond to the prompting of the Holy Spirit to

All that God has done, even in the midst of the desolation season, has a purpose and will work together to move us into what He has for us in our new place.

align ourselves with God's mind and connect with His heart so that we can move forward. This can only happen by communicating with a holy, sovereign God. As we come into agreement with God through His intercessory call to us, He will propel us out of our desolate circumstances and move us into prophetic fulfillment.

In Ezekiel 22, God was ready to restore the people of Judah. In verses 23-29, God describes how the priests had been unholy, the prophets had been conspirators, the government officials had been like ravenous wolves, and the people had fallen into

divination. Nevertheless, in verse 30, God says that if He can find one person who will make a wall and stand in the gap before Him on behalf of the land, He will reverse everything the prophets, priests and government officials had done wrong. He even promised to reverse the sinful corruption into which the people had fallen. He would do all of this if He could just find someone to meet with Him.

Intercession is defined as reaching or meeting someone to pressure them strongly to change a situation. Hebrews 7:25 states of Jesus, "Therefore He is also able to save to the uttermost those who come to God through Him, since He always lives to make intercession for them." Christ is available to us to make intercession for us. This is what an intercessory call is all about. The Spirit of God will co-labor with us and reveal our plan of escape and the way out of desolation. But we must be willing to pray. We must be willing to meet with God until we gain strategy for moving forward and then take a stand against the enemy who would seek to keep us bound in desolation. If we do this, God will not only break us out of our desolation, but He will also bring us out of whatever corruption we may have fallen into in our place of desolation. He will cleanse, renew and restore us to a place of communion with Him.

Step Two: God Revives Unfulfilled Prophetic Destiny

As we come into agreement with God through intercession, He often reminds us of His plan of prophetic destiny. Daniel discovered this when he had to go back 70 years to find out what God had promised the people of Israel. The prophet Jeremiah had prophesied that the whole land would go into desolation and serve the King of Babylon for 70 years (see Jer. 25:11). As Daniel received the prayer burden from God, he was able to understand this word that Jeremiah the prophet had spoken. It was now time for the power of desolation to be broken and for restoration to begin!

That's how it is with us many times. Some of our grandparents and great grandparents had incredible prophetic destinies that were never realized. We need to understand how their prophetic inheritance became captive to the enemy. We also need to understand how the generational blessings of God have not been fulfilled.

I had to come to an understanding of unfulfilled prophetic destiny in my own life by watching my father. My father was a man who had a great deal of potential. However, he made bad choices. The path he chose for himself had corruption and defilement. Instead of glorifying God, his path ended with him dying a premature death. His destiny was never fulfilled.

God has created each one of us to reflect His glory. When we understand our identity in Him and begin to come into the fullness of that identity, His glory is seen through us. The absence of His glory indicates a curse. A curse working in our life brings desolation and postponement to the fulfillment of His promises. By seeing the mess that my father had made of his own life, and even by being abused by his hand, I could have said, "O woe is me, look at what my father did." Instead I found myself saying, "Look at what my father could have been. Look at what he could have accomplished had he allowed God to bring him into His ultimate plan for his life. Look at what should have been."

The Lord even once revealed to me the overwhelming love that He had for my earthly father. When I saw how much God loved him and what an incredible plan He had for my father's life, I immediately said, "Lord, let me not only come into the fullness of my own life, but let me accomplish the things that were meant for my father in his generation that were sent astray by his alignment with the enemy."

I have learned, as we will discuss further in chapter 5, that prophetic destiny is often tied to the generations of our families. I therefore want to be sure that I somehow complete what God

has intended for my bloodline. I need to become successful where there has been failure in my family. I need to overcome the enemy where others in my bloodline have not withstood him. To have prophetic fulfillment in our own lives, we need to allow the Lord to revive the unfulfilled prophetic destiny in our family line and give us a success mentality of completion and fulfillment.

Step Three: God Calls Us to Prophesy into Our Destiny

As hard as it is for many to believe, God has chosen to use us as a necessary link to bring His will to Earth. He calls us to come into dialogue with Him, listen to His voice and gain prophetic revelation so that the hope of our calling can be fulfilled. He asks us to take that revelation and prophesy it into the earthly realm.

This action of declaring prophetic revelation is called *prophetic intercession*. Barbara Wentroble states, "Prophetic intercession is one type of prayer that unlocks miracles and releases the blessings of God. . . . The Body of Christ stands today in the womb of the dawn of a new day (see Ps. 110:3). We are birthing prayers that have the power to break through."[3]

According to Cindy Jacobs, "prophetic intercession is an urging to pray given by the Holy Spirit. . . . You pray for the prayer requests that are on the heart of God. He nudges you to pray so that He can intervene. . . . God will direct you to pray to bring forth His will on the earth as it is His will in heaven."[4] In other words, God says, *"Here is what I plan to do in this area—now prophesy it."*

PROPHESYING OUR DESTINY

Throughout the Bible, we see examples of God's people making these types of prophetic declarations into their situations in order to see His will come about. Such was the case in Ezekiel 36 and 37. God said to Ezekiel:

But I had concern for My holy name, which the house of Israel had profaned among the nations wherever they went. Therefore say to the house of Israel, "Thus says the Lord GOD: 'I do not do this for your sake, O house of Israel, but for My holy name's sake, which you have profaned among the nations wherever you went. And I will sanctify My great name, which has been profaned among the nations, which you have profaned in their midst; and the nations shall know that I am the LORD,' says the Lord GOD, 'when I am hallowed in you before their eyes. For I will take you from among the nations, gather you out of all countries, and bring you into your own land'" (Ezek. 36:21-24).

There was a process of scattering that had occurred among God's people. Satan knows how to scatter us and draw us into his process of division and scattering. So what the Lord told Ezekiel was that even though Israel (signified by the bones in Ezekiel 37) had been scattered, He was going to bring them back together. God then gave Ezekiel an understanding of Israel's prophetic destiny that he was to declare into the earth:

The hand of the LORD came upon me and brought me out in the Spirit of the LORD, and set me down in the midst of the valley; and it was full of bones. Then He caused me to pass by them all around, and behold, there were very many in the open valley; and indeed they were very dry. And He said to me, "Son of man, can these bones live?" So I answered, "O Lord GOD, You know." Again He said to me, "Prophesy to these bones, and say to them, 'O dry bones, hear the word of the LORD! Thus says the Lord GOD to these bones: "Surely I will cause breath to enter into you, and you shall live. I will put

sinews on you and bring flesh upon you, cover you with skin and put breath in you; and you shall live. Then you shall know that I am the LORD" ' " (Ezek. 37:1-6).

There are four levels of prophetic declaration in Ezekiel 37 that can help us to understand the process of prophetic fulfillment. In each level, there comes a place where prophetic fulfillment can stall. Understanding how the process can stall will help us proceed into the next dimension of prophetic fulfillment.

Level One: Coming Together

"So I prophesied as I was commanded; and as I prophesied, there was a noise, and suddenly a rattling; and the bones came together, bone to bone. Indeed, as I looked, the sinews and the flesh came upon them, and the skin covered them over" (Ezek. 37:7-8).

Ezekiel took the words that God gave him and declared them into the desolate situation that had overtaken Judah. This is what is meant by *prophetic declaration*. When Ezekiel declared God's will, things began to happen. The same is true with us. When we see God's prophetic destiny in our lives and begin to declare it, something will happen. However, we have to release faith before we can see the results with our eyes. Sometimes we look for results without releasing faith, but it simply does not work that way. Faith comes first.

When Ezekiel first prophesied, there was a rattling noise and the bones came together, and then the sinews and flesh covered the bones. In the first level of prophecy, when we prophecy what God has promised us, we hear a new sound and see a new structure coming together. We even gain a portion of the plan to move forward. However, just having a plan is not enough.

Level Two: The Breath of Life

"But there was no breath in them. Also He said to me, 'Prophesy to the breath, prophesy, son of man, and say to the breath, "Thus says the Lord GOD: 'Come from the four winds, O breath, and breathe on these slain, that they may live'"'" (Ezek. 37:8-9).

Here we see the second level of prophecy. Ezekiel had seen the bones come together and the flesh appear, but there was no breath in them. There was no life. Did that mean he was a false prophet? No, of course not. It just meant that something was not yet working to produce prophetic fulfillment. So the Lord said, "Go back and prophesy to that part that has not received life." Notice that He did not tell Ezekiel to re-prophesy everything from the beginning, but only to prophesy to the part that was not working and command it to come in line with God's plans and purposes.

When we encounter a snag in declaring God's word, it does not necessarily mean that we have not heard God or that we have failed. It often means that we need to enter into a second level of prophecy in order to see life come into that which God is longing to bring to life.

Level Three: Spiritual Warfare over Hope Deferred

"So I prophesied as He commanded me, and breath came into them, and they lived, and stood upon their feet, an exceedingly great army. Then He said to me, 'Son of man, these bones are the whole house of Israel. They indeed say, "Our bones are dry, our hope is lost, and we ourselves are cut off!"'" (Ezek. 37:10-11).

Ezekiel saw a great army result from his prophetic declarations. But as those in the army began to speak, they said that they were filled with despair. When we become filled with despair, our faith for the future can easily be depleted. Lost hope often works with rejection and causes us to feel isolated and cut off, as was the case with this great army in Ezekiel 37. According

to Proverbs 13:12, hope deferred makes the heart sick and releases a spirit of infirmity.

Ezekiel had seen great and miraculous things happen as a result of his prophetic declarations. Yet there was still hopelessness and infirmity. When this happens in our lives, we need to enter into a third level of prophecy: *spiritual warfare*. It is not enough to have flesh and breath. We must fight against whatever the enemy is doing to try to steal the life that God has breathed into our destiny. If we don't engage in spiritual warfare and overturn the enemy's plans to cause death, we won't progress and overturn the spirit of infirmity that has entered and is resisting our prophetic fulfillment.

Hope deferred causes much sickness. There is a place in the fulfillment of the promise of God over our lives in which we have to deal with the past issues that have come against us to discourage and defeat us. Notice that the bones in Ezekiel 37 had to express the hope deferred that was within them. Don't be afraid to face the problems of your past. By dealing with these past issues, you will be released to move into the hope for the future.

Level Four: Hope for the Future

"Therefore prophesy and say to them, 'Thus says the Lord GOD: "Behold, O My people, I will open your graves and cause you to come up from your graves, and bring you into the land of Israel. Then you shall know that I am the LORD, when I have opened your graves, O My people, and brought you up from your graves. I will put My Spirit in you, and you shall live, and I will place you in your own land. Then you shall know that I, the LORD, have spoken it and performed it," says the LORD'" (Ezek. 37:12-14).

Notice that the phrase "I will place you in your own land" was the prophetic destiny released in Ezekiel 36. The word of the Lord had come full circle! But what if Ezekiel had stopped pressing forward after the bones had come together and there was no

breath? That's what we tend to do in the Body of Christ. We think that we've heard God and we prophesy; but when things don't turn out as we thought, we give up and end up falling short of reaching our prophetic destiny. We do not see the word that God has spoken to us being manifest and fulfilled. As Ezekiel prophesied at the fourth level, resurrection power was released so that the graves could be opened and the people brought in their own land. I love the phrase "Then you will know that I, the LORD, have *spoken it* and *performed it*, says the LORD" (v. 14, emphasis added).

It's one thing to have a promise in your life that you know is from God, but it's another thing for that promise to be performed in your life. In Ezekiel 37, four levels of agreement and prophesying were necessary to see the fulfillment of God's word. We cannot be a people that faint easily. Discouragement has no place in us as God's people. If we choose not to back up but to keep moving forward through the levels of prophecy, then God will perform His will in us and bring about prophetic fulfillment!

FORTY DAYS OR FORTY YEARS?

God has a cycle of life for each of us. This life cycle begins at conception and moves along in the following progression:

1. *Conception:* God begins His purpose for us by knitting us together in the womb.
2. *Birth:* The new life that God has created is brought forth.
3. *Age of accountability*: We gain an awareness of our need for God.
4. *Rebirth*: We are quickened from darkness into light.
5. *Receiving hope*: We search for and receive the expectation of God for our future.
6. *Maturing of our faith:* Our faith is matured into an overcoming weapon of God.

7. *Demonstration:* God demonstrates His power and wisdom, which unlocks our destiny.
8. *Manifestation:* God manifests His glory and inner fulfillment of our identity in Him.
9. *Completion:* Our role in the early realm is completed as we face death and enter into eternity.

The enemy loves to interrupt the life cycle in any one of these stages so that the fulfillment of our destiny cannot be completed. He would love for us to miss the *kairos* or opportune time

We all have wilderness seasons that are ordained of God in which we move from one season to another.

that the Lord has in each of these phases above. However, if you miss that *now* time, it doesn't mean that things will never be back in order. It just means that you will postpone what God wants to do and enter into a prolonged wilderness season.

We all have wilderness seasons that are ordained of God in which we move from one season to another. However, we can prolong this wilderness season. Jesus stayed in His wilderness season for 40 days, whereas the Israelites stayed in their wilderness season for 40 years (see Mark 1:13; Num. 14:33-34). The Israelites were held captive in their wilderness season because of their unbelief and hardness of heart, whereas Jesus resisted the devil in His wilderness season and came out of it filled with power for His future.

The choice is ours! If we are willing to press toward our prophetic fulfillment in God's time, our season of desolation will not be prolonged. However, if we, like the Israelites, allow the enemy to overcome us with discouragement, hopelessness

and a lack of faith, we too may find ourselves in a prolonged season of desolation that leaves us wandering for many years.

As we mentioned at the beginning of this chapter, prophetic fulfillment can often seem to mess up our lives. In fact, we may even feel that everything has been turned upside down. But it is in prophetic fulfillment that we reach God's destiny for our lives. As you come face to face with your own prophetic destiny in God's *now* time for your life, *you* must determine in your own heart if your wandering season will last for 40 days or for 40 years.

PROPHETIC DECLARATION

Declarations have power! Here is a prophetic declaration that will help you unlock the next level of fulfillment of God's purpose in your life:

> *I declare that God has a purpose for my life. I receive wisdom and revelation over the hope of my calling. I declare that every strategy of hell that has interrupted God's plan for my life will be exposed. I declare that every hindrance that has stopped me from progressing will be revealed and that I will advance in God's plan for my life. I declare that my faith will be stirred. I declare that new strength will come into my spirit. And I declare that the wilderness will blossom and God's glory will be seen in my life! I declare that the best is yet ahead!*

Notes

1. Dutch Sheets, *God's Timing for Your Life* (Ventura, CA: Regal Books, 2001), pp. 17-18. Emphasis in original.
2. Ibid., pp. 18-19.
3. Barbara Wentroble, *Prophetic Intercession* (Ventura, CA: Regal Books, 2003), p. 27.
4. Cindy Jacobs, *Possessing the Gates of the Enemy* (Tarrytown, NY: Chosen Books, 1991), pp. 146-147.

Seven Issues of Prophetic Fulfillment

*For wisdom is better than rubies, and all the things one
may desire cannot be compared with her.*

PROVERBS 8:11

As we discussed in the last chapter, prophetic fulfillment is not
an automatic occurrence in our lives. Of course, God is sovereign and can do anything, but most of the time He does not
override the decisions we make for ourselves and, good or bad,
we must live with the consequences of those decisions. The
wonderful thing about the Lord is that even when we stray, if
we listen, He will provide ways for us to get back into His ultimate plan. Therefore, we must learn how to participate with

His will for prophetic fulfillment to take place.

The word "fulfill" means to bring something into actuality. It can also mean to carry out and order, to measure up, to satisfy, to bring to an end or to complete. So, prophetic fulfillment means that the will and heart of God for our life, and all that He intends for us, is complete. In other words, His desire for our life is fully manifested. In this chapter, we will outline seven vital issues that we need to understand to help keep us on course as we move in God's full plan for our lives.

Issue One:
We must know what God is saying to us and then say "yes and amen" to His promises for us.

"For all the promises of God in Him are Yes, and in Him Amen, to the glory of God through us" (2 Cor. 1:20). Sadly, many Christians will die without ever having fulfilled their prophetic destiny. This is not necessarily because of sin in their lives; often, it is because they never learned to hear God's voice and understand where He was trying to lead. They end up groping in the dark, unable to obey the Lord because they do not comprehend what He requires in order for them to move toward their destiny.

Even if we have a good idea of where God wants us to move, the path toward that destination is usually very different than we imagined. Countless times I have heard comments such as "I knew God would do this, but I never imagined it would be this way!" That is why it is so important for us to hear God at every step along the way.

One key principle for saying yes and amen to God's promises is continuing to look forward rather than looking back. Hanging on to what has already slipped away from us accomplishes nothing and can even cloud our vision of what lies ahead. Many people stop moving toward their future because they hang

on to their past. For true prophetic fulfillment, we must grab on to what God is doing now. We need to say, "Lord, what are You doing with me *today*? What are You trying to move me into so that I can reconnect and bring about that which You are trying to do for my future?"

Once we have come into an understanding of God's promises for our lives, we need to acknowledge these promises with yes and amen. This means that we need to actually verbalize it to God and to others. Confession of our mouth is tremendously important: "For it is with your heart that you believe and are justified, and it is with your mouth that you confess and are saved" (Rom. 10:10, *NIV*). The word "confess" in this verse means "harmonious" or "together." Therefore, by verbalizing God's promises for us, we are actually coming into harmonious agreement together with Him. This act builds our faith and shuts the door to Satan's lies.

What comes out of our mouths is vitally important. "Not what goes into the mouth defiles a man; but what comes out of the mouth, this defiles a man" (Matt. 15:11). We have both the power of salvation and the power of defilement in the words that we choose to speak. Our confessions could mean the difference between receiving prophetic fulfillment and missing our destiny. For this reason, we must come into agreement by verbally saying yes and amen to God's promises for us.

I want to be quick to add one note of caution when it comes to verbalizing what we believe God's promises are for our lives. We must be careful to let the Lord give us wisdom over who to tell and what to say. Otherwise, we may end up in a mess, just as Joseph was when he bragged about his dream to his brothers and they became so angry that they sold him into slavery! It is often a matter of timing. Broadcasting something that is meant to be kept on a shelf or in a prayer closet is the spiritual equivalent of the old wartime adage "loose lips sink ships!"

Issue Two:
The promise that God has for us must be incorporated into the overall destiny for ourselves and for others.

"And if one member suffers, all the members suffer with it; or if one member is honored, all the members rejoice with it" (1 Cor. 12:26). God does nothing independent of whatever else He is trying to accomplish. In other words, whatever He is trying to do in your life fits into a bigger picture.

In a society such as ours that places high value on individual achievement, it is often hard for us to understand that our destiny is linked to others and that we will not succeed alone. We are connected one to another. Therefore, the promises that God has for our lives are being incorporated into a greater destiny of which we are a part. Our promises are linked to the overall movement of God not only in our lives, but also in our territories and in generations past and yet to come. Even though God is a very personal God, He enacts our promises along with those of others to whom He has connected us. If either we or those other individuals are not asking God to work out our promises, we all suffer. (This is an issue that we will discuss in greater detail in chapter 5.)

Issue Three:
We must be in a process of receiving prophetic revelation.

Our life and destiny are on a continuum. As we move through life, we need to constantly seek new direction and new revelation from God. We can't just grab a hold of one level of revelation and think that it's going to ride us through to the end. In the last chapter, we discussed the four levels of prophecy that Ezekiel had to move through in order to see God accomplish all that He intended to in the valley of dry bones. If Ezekiel had stopped at

any point before God's full purpose had been accomplished, he would have failed. Ezekiel went through a four-step process at each new level of prophecy. These are the same four steps that we need to follow if we want to stay on track with prophetic fulfillment in our own lives.

Step One: He received prophetic revelation. Ezekiel sought God and was open to receiving prophetic instruction. In fact, he *expected* God to speak to him. How often in our daily lives do we expect to hear God? God is speaking to us today! We need to learn how to listen for God's voice in order to receive the direction for our lives that will move us forward.

Step Two: He obeyed the voice of the Lord. God told Ezekiel what to say and what to do in order for the next step to be accomplished. This seems so basic, yet it is a critical step that we must understand. Ezekiel could not have moved to the fourth level of prophecy without first obeying God at the first, second and third levels. If you are having difficulty gaining new revelation and hearing the voice of the Lord, go back and be sure that you have done all that the Lord has required of you thus far. For example, if you have fallen out of relationship with someone and the Lord reveals that you have to get right with that person, don't go back to the Lord looking for new revelation until you have obeyed Him in the last revelation. If you want to continue to move forward toward prophetic fulfillment, you had better go get right with that person.

> If you are having difficulty gaining new revelation and hearing the voice of the Lord, go back and be sure that you have done all that the Lord has required of you thus far.

Step Three: He watched God's purpose being accomplished and assessed the situation. At each level of obedience, Ezekiel saw miracles happen as God's will was accomplished. Even so, he knew that all of God's purposes had not yet been fulfilled. He saw the bones come together—which in itself must have been a great and miraculous sight—but when he looked closer, he saw that even with this great miracle, there was no breath in the bones. Then he saw breath come into them and a great army of living, breathing beings replaced a dead pile of dry, useless bones. And yet there was still hopelessness and infirmity. It was not until Ezekiel saw the Lord break infirmity and death off of the great army and bring them into the land that He had promised for them that the process of prophetic fulfillment was complete. Even though we may see great miracles along the way, we need to be sensitive to the Holy Spirit's leading as to whether or not His will has been fully accomplished.

Step Four: He listened for his next instruction. Miracle after miracle did not stop Ezekiel from seeking God for the next step. Ezekiel did not bask in the awesome works of God in a way that prevented him from looking forward. Of course, we need to stop and thank God for His great power and allow ourselves to be drawn into worship. But we can't let the glory of something that has already occurred keep us from moving toward a greater level of glory.

Have you ever tried to walk backward while focusing on where you have just been? Not only is your progress greatly slowed, you are also liable to fall on an obstacle that you should have seen. Remember, Jesus "steadfastly set His face to go to Jerusalem" (Luke 9:51). He never got off track in His purposes on Earth, and by staying totally focused, He brought the redemption to us. We need to keep our eyes focused on what lies ahead and seek God for our next instructions. Even with all of Paul's great accomplishments for the Lord, he writes, "I do not

count myself to have apprehended; but one thing I do, forgetting those things which are behind and reaching forward to those things which are ahead, I press toward the goal for the prize of the upward call of God in Christ Jesus" (Phil. 3:13-14). Paul was reaching toward his prophetic fulfillment.

Issue Four:
We must learn to engage in warfare
with our prophecies.

"This charge I commit to you, son Timothy, according to the prophecies previously made concerning you, that by them you may wage the good warfare" (1 Tim. 1:18). Receiving a prophetic revelation from God about what He wants to accomplish does not mean it's a done deal. There is a conditional nature to prophecy that involves both our obedience and our willingness to wage "war" with a prophetic word. Because this is such a critical issue in prophetic fulfillment, all of chapter 3 will be devoted to this subject.

Issue Five:
We must have our authority and accountability
structures in place for prophetic fulfillment.

The issue of proper authority and alignment in our lives cannot be omitted or even understated when it comes to prophetic fulfillment. This biblical principle is brought up over and over again in topics such as parents over children, masters over slaves, employers over employees, the priesthood over the people, and so forth. Watchman Nee said it this way:

> We should not be occupied with right or wrong, good or
> evil; rather should we know who is the authority above us.

Once we learn to whom we must be subject, we naturally
find our place in the body. Alas, how many Christians
today have not the faintest idea concerning subjection.
No wonder there is so much confusion and disorder. . . .
Obedience is a foundational principle. If this matter of
authority remains unsolved, nothing can be solved. As
faith is the principle by which we obtain life, so obedience
is the principle by which that life is lived out.[1]

We will never reach prophetic fulfillment as loners. Even
though we can be right with God and end up in heaven, fulfillment on Earth will not occur if we lack an understanding of
authority. If we are to be victorious in our lives, we cannot side-
step the Bible. Therefore, we need to understand the role that
authority plays in our lives. The following are some important
factors to consider in being properly aligned under the authority God that has placed in our lives.

Mentoring. Despite the fact that my earthly father was not
a good representation of the Lord, God has always seen to it that
there have been spiritual fathers in my life who provided mentoring and guidance. After my dad died, God put a natural uncle
in my life. Then my mother met a wonderful man who later
became my stepfather and gave me clear direction to attend
Texas A&M University. The Lord then put a key pastor in my life,
then a mission leader, and then a wonderful apostolic leader
with whom I am aligned, C. Peter Wagner. I have always coveted
these relationships and submitted to them.

But not all authority in my life has been from men. There
have been many women in my life whom I also consider to be
spiritual authorities and to whom I have submitted. My mother
and grandmother were certainly in that category. God placed a
godly woman named LaCelia Henderson in my life after I was
baptized in the Holy Spirit to teach me about spiritual life. In

more recent years, I have had the privilege of being mentored by Doris Wagner, a wonderful administrator, as I have served under her at Global Harvest Ministries. All those who have mentored me, both men and women, have played crucial roles in my own prophetic fulfillment.

Discipline. Submitting to authority always brings discipline into our lives. In this context, the word "discipline" does not mean punishment, but rather an inward strength and a pathway by which God can work in our lives. In his classic book *Celebration of Discipline*, Richard J. Foster says, "God has given us [discipline] of spiritual life as a means of receiving his grace. [Discipline] allows us to place ourselves before God so that he can transform us."[2] My brother, Keith, simply puts it this way: "Discipline defines the gift."

Freedom. I love this verse: "And now look, I free you this day from the chains that were on your hand. If it seems good to you to come with me to Babylon, come, and I will look after you. But if it seems wrong for you to come with me to Babylon, remain here. See, all the land is before you; wherever it seems good and convenient for you to go, go there" (Jer. 40:4). In other words, after Jeremiah had done what the Lord had asked him to do, he was granted the freedom to choose where he would go in the days ahead. The word "freedom" means to open wide, loosen, release, untie, unshackle or liberate. It often refers to opening one's hand, eyes or mouth. Richard Foster states:

> Every Discipline has its corresponding freedom. What freedom corresponds to submission? It is the ability to lay down the terrible burden of always needing to get our own way. The obsession to demand that things go the way we want them to go is one of the greatest bondages of human society. . . . In submission we are at last free to value other people. Their dreams and plans become

important to us. . . . For the first time we can love people unconditionally."[3]

As mentioned earlier, our prophetic destinies are always linked to what God is working to accomplish in the lives of those with whom we are connected, in the territories in which we live, and in the generations past and yet to come. As we submit to authority, we gain the freedom to see God's bigger plan and understand the part that we are called to play in that plan. Understanding authority in our lives does indeed bring freedom.

Order. Everything God created has order. One of Satan's chief goals is to counteract the works of God by thwarting His order. Therefore, Satan works to bring disunity, mistrust, confusion, disobedience, ineffectiveness and, ultimately, destruction by breaking down God's structure of authority. As we choose to submit to God's authority structures in our lives, we restore and maintain God's plan of order and make great strides toward prophetic fulfillment.

God has a prototype of order for the Church. First Corinthians 12:28 states, "And God has appointed these in the church: first apostles, second prophets, third teachers, and after that miracles." This does not mean that each gift operates outside of its own authority; it means that until each of these gifts are properly aligned, we will not see God's model of what He has in heaven manifested on Earth. That's how order works. Once we come into order (which is a military term), we are aligned properly for victory.

Covering. The word "covering" means "protection, concealing, warmth, hidden from view or being in a place of safety." Being in proper alignment with authority produces these things in our lives. If we remain under our place of authority, the enemy has far fewer available means of attacking us because we are

covered or hidden from his view. Psalm 91 is a beautiful example of covering as we remain under the authority of the Lord:

> He who dwells in the secret place of the Most High shall abide under the shadow of the Almighty. I will say of the LORD, "He is my refuge and my fortress; my God, in Him I will trust." Surely He shall deliver you from the snare of the fowler and from the perilous pestilence. He shall cover you with His feathers, and under His wings you shall take refuge; His truth shall be your shield and buckler. You shall not be afraid of the terror by night, nor of the arrow that flies by day (vv. 1-5).

Clarity. God often gives those in authority over us a supernatural insight into our lives. Their wisdom and counsel can provide the clarity of vision to move forward that we may not possess in and of ourselves. Of course, we need to weigh their advice with the discernment that God has given to us and be careful of those who may try to abuse their authority by controlling us. Nevertheless, we must be open to receiving God's clarity and wisdom through our authority structures.

Connections. Many times, our destiny does not come about because we are not connected properly to others in the Body of Christ. As we noted before, Watchman Nee said, "Once we learn to whom we must be subject, we naturally find our place in the body."[4] There are incredible connections of people in the Bible that brought about the fulfillment of God's purposes. In the Old Testament, Deborah and Barak were one such connection; Esther and Mordechai were another. In the New Testament, Paul and Barnabas represented this connection, and Peter's destiny was fulfilled when Andrew connected him with Jesus. Jesus then began to prophesy into Peter's life the full redemption plan that God had for him (see John 1:51).

God's prophetic purpose for our lives and our territories requires us to be connected to one another. We need to know with whom God has sovereignly linked us, maintain strong alliances with those people, and respect those in authority over us. Understanding and maintaining proper connections is another way to destroy Satan's schemes, because he will have a difficult time infiltrating our ranks.

Healing. "Is anyone among you sick? Let him call for the elders of the church, and let them pray over him, anointing him with oil in the name of the Lord" (Jas. 5:14). During the season when my wife, Pam, was being healed of barrenness, there came a time when she went to our pastor and asked that he pray for her, which he did. I honestly believe that the barrenness would not have been broken from her if she had not been obedient to the Bible's admonition in James 5. When she submitted herself to biblical authority by asking for prayer, a progression of events began that liberated and healed her.

Faith. In our book *The Future War of the Church*, Rebecca and I explain the link between authority and faith:

> The Lord showed me that if I would begin to understand and analyze every authority that had influence in my life, I would begin to operate in a new level of faith. Faith is linked with authority. To the extent that we submit to the authority God has placed in our lives, our faith has the opportunity to be stretched and strengthened. Faith is the overcoming agent that God's people have on this Earth (see John 14:12); therefore, if the Church is to overcome, we must understand and submit to proper authority.[5]

Power. Being in proper alignment with authority, both those in authority over us and those to whom we are an authority, is a key to power. In Matthew 8, there is a story of a centurion who

pled with Jesus to heal his sick servant: "The centurion answered and said, 'Lord, I am not worthy that You should come under my roof. But only speak a word, and my servant will be healed. For I also am a man under authority, having soldiers under me'" (Matt.

Prophetic fulfillment is a process— sometimes a very long process that can test our ability to persevere and believe that God will do all that He promised.

8:8-9). This centurion was able to seek out the Lord and gain healing for his servant because he submitted to the Lord's authority and used his own authority to ask healing for someone underneath him. His understanding of where he stood in the authority structure gave him power to help those under him.

Issue Six:
We must have a persevering spirit to break through.

Prophetic fulfillment is a process—sometimes a very long process that can test our ability to persevere and believe that God will do all that He promised. Hell doesn't want you to break through. It takes perseverance to break through the processes of hell that have been set against your promise and your destiny. Therefore, always try to stay close to God so that you can persevere in those hard times. I love the way my dear friend Barbara Yoder describes persevering for breakthrough in her book *The Breaker Anointing*:

God has a great deal for us to possess, but taking possession will require great faith and perseverance. God is continually putting new challenges before us to develop

our faith and perseverance at a deeper level. We must continually remind ourselves of what God instructed the Israelites in Judges 3:1-4:

> Now these are the nations which the LORD left, that He might test Israel by them, that is, all who had not known any of the wars in Canaan (this was only so that the generations of the children of Israel might be taught to know war, at least those who had not formerly known it), namely, five lords of the Philistines, all the Canaanites, the Sidonians, and the Hivites who dwelt in Mount Lebanon, from Mount Baal Hermon to the entrance of Hamath. And they were left, that He might test Israel by them, to know whether they would obey the commandments of the LORD, which He had commanded their fathers by the hand of Moses.

We may decide to quit at some point because a gate seems unconquerable. We may be tired and weary of the battle. We may want to sit down, take a rest and check out. We have the option of sitting down and living a life of ease. However, if we do so, we will never reach our potential because fear or weariness has overtaken us at the threshold. When we make this decision, we fail to reach our destiny.

Paul said that he kept pressing on to attain that for which he had been apprehended to attain (see Phil. 3:12-14). God had apprehended Paul not just to convert him but also to use him to accomplish a great ministry—to take the gospel to the Gentiles in many nations. Paul pressed through despite many trials.[6]

Issue Seven:
Prophetic fulfillment requires humility.

As we have seen throughout this chapter, we will not reach our destinies apart from one another. We are dependant on each other for prophetic fulfillment. There is no room for pride in the equation. This also keeps us humble, knowing that unless God infuses us with strength, power and wisdom, we cannot break forth. God is only going to use humble and holy people to build His kingdom in days ahead. In a recent teaching that C. Peter Wagner delivered on humility, he quoted the following from Andrew Murray:

> We need only think for a moment what faith is. Is it not the confession of nothingness and helplessness, the surrender and the waiting to let God work? Is it not in itself the most humbling thing there can be—the acceptance of our place as dependents, who can claim or get or do nothing but what grace bestows?[7]

We can never reach our destiny, nor even draw our next breath, apart from the grace and mercy of God. No matter what our prophetic promises may be, let us never come to the place where we forget that we are only dust that has experienced the touch of God. It is only through Him and through those with whom He has connected us that we will ever accomplish the purpose for which He has fashioned us!

Notes

1. Watchman Nee, *Spiritual Authority* (New York: Christian Fellowship Publishers Inc., 1972), p. 23.
2. Richard J. Foster, *Celebration of Discipline* (San Francisco: Harper and Row Publishers, 1988), p. 7.
3. Ibid. pp. 111-112.

4. Watchman Nee, *Spiritual Authority*, p. 23.

5. Chuck D. Pierce and Rebecca Wagner Sytsema, *The Future War of the Church* (Ventura, CA: Regal Books, 2001), p. 32.

6. Barbara Yoder, *The Breaker Anointing* (Ventura, CA: Regal Books, 2001), pp. 53-54.

7. Andrew Murray, *Humility* (New Kensington, PA: Whitaker House, 1982), p. 68.

Warring with a Prophetic Word

> *This charge I commit to you, son Timothy, according to the prophecies previously made concerning you, that by them you may wage the good warfare.*
>
> 1 TIMOTHY 1:18

Up to this point, we have talked a great deal about destiny and prophetic fulfillment, but we have not discussed prophecy itself. This chapter is devoted to understanding the role that prophecy plays in our lives and how to wage warfare with the prophecies we receive.

UNDERSTANDING PERSONAL PROPHECY

The simple definition of prophecy is speaking forth the mind and heart of God under the inspiration of the Holy Spirit.

Therefore, to give an accurate word of God, we must have both His mind and His emotion as we deliver that word. A prophetic declaration communicates God's intent to fulfill His promises to us. Receiving a prophetic word can have a powerful impact on the perception of our prophetic destiny. This word can help shape our vision for the future and bring us into a deeper understanding of God's heart for our lives.

In our book *Receiving the Word of the Lord*, Rebecca and I discuss more fully the value, process and function of prophecy, and we offer several ways to test a prophetic word. *Receiving the Word of the Lord* will help anyone who needs a basic explanation of personal prophecy. In the context of this book, however, we want to focus on prophecy as it pertains to prophetic fulfillment. In order to do this, we first need to take a closer look at several aspects of how prophecy works in our lives.[1]

We need to be sensitive to God's development that will provide the fertile soil in which prophetic fulfillment will blossom to its fullest.

Prophecy Is Incomplete

"For we know in part and we prophesy in part" (1 Cor. 13:9). No personal or corporate word of prophecy is complete in and of itself. In his excellent book *Developing Your Prophetic Gifting*, Graham Cooke says, "God only reveals what we need to know in order to do his will in that particular time and place. The things that he does not wish us to know, he keeps secret from the one prophesying. Elisha said, 'The Lord has hidden it from me!' (2 Kings 4:27). In other words, 'I don't know.'"[2]

Cooke goes on to say, "Oddly enough, a prophecy will give us positive highlights about our future role or tasks, but may say

nothing about any pitfalls we may encounter. It may not refer to enemy opposition, people letting us down, or any crushing disappointments that we may experience as we attempt to be faithful to our call."[3]

God may give us a little bit of revelation here and a little bit there. In retrospect, we may wonder why God didn't tell us this or that, or why He did tell us some seemingly unimportant detail. But God always knows what He is doing when He reveals His heart to us through prophecy. This is something that we must simply trust. We must bear in mind, however, that we do not know all that we may encounter or how the prophecies will be fulfilled. Prophecy may point out a path, but we must follow the Lord daily and trust in Him as we move along that path. Prophetic fulfillment comes in moving down the path that was pointed out through personal prophecy.

Prophecy Evolves

As we follow the Lord in obedience, He will give us the next piece of revelation. He will not tell us what He wants us to do three steps down the road, but will give each piece to us step by step. Such was the case with Abraham. God gave him a piece here and a piece there. Each time Abraham obeyed, God would speak to him to confirm and expand the prophecy that had been given to him, give him new insights, and move him on to his next place. One exciting dimension of Abraham's prophetic evolution occurred in Genesis 22 when God revealed Himself as Jehovah Jireh to Abraham. This name for God actually means that God will reveal provision we can't see so that we can advance into our future. Another tremendous concept in this chapter was that God prophesied the next piece of Abraham's destiny into his son Isaac. Therefore, what Abraham could not accomplish or complete was passed on to the next generation.

This is the way of prophecy. Each prophetic word is incomplete, yet as we faithfully obey God, we receive new pieces of the puzzle. Recent prophecies will often build on earlier ones to bring confirmation and fresh understanding. Cooke writes, "The Lord will never speak the totality of his heart to us in a single prophetic word. Rather he speaks words that will give us a focus for now and the immediate future. As we work within those prophecies and allow our lives to be encouraged and shaped by them, we can see that prophecy builds from one word to another."[4]

Prophecy Is Conditional

The key to the process of prophecy is obedience. God will not usurp our wills and force us to follow His will. Mary, for instance, could have said no to the prophetic pronouncement that she would become pregnant. Instead, she responded by saying, "Behold the maidservant of the Lord! Let it be to me according to your word" (Luke 1:38). Had she said no to the prophecy, the Holy Spirit would never have forced her to become pregnant!

Although Mary did not completely understand how she would become pregnant nor grasp the magnitude of what she had been chosen for, she nevertheless knew that through the prophetic word, God had revealed His destiny for her life. Through her choice of obedience, the word came to pass and the human race gained access to its full redemptive plan.

The condition of obedience to the Holy Spirit is not a negotiable factor in prophetic fulfillment. In the *New King James Version* of the Old Testament, the word "faith" is used only twice. However, the concept of faith was built into the obedience of God's people based upon the promise that He had spoken to them. As God's people obeyed, they became the fathers and mothers of our faith. Therefore, when God's word comes to us, we should always look for the obedience factor.

As mentioned in the last chapter, just because we have received a prophetic word does not mean it is a done deal. We are often tempted to believe that the fulfillment of a prophetic word is the next step in our lives, but there may be some things that we have to do first in obedience to God. Abraham, for instance, had to be circumcised before he saw prophetic fulfillment (see Gen. 17:23). And then there was that big event where he had to put Isaac, his only son, on the altar (see Gen. 22:1-19). "Only son" meant that Abraham's entire future was wrapped up in this individual. However, this was the condition that God had placed on him before He could reveal and extend His promise to the next generation.

Let us add one note of clarification: There is some prophecy that is unconditional and that God alone will fulfill. God is sovereign. He can do anything He wishes. But usually in His plan, He makes it provisional for us to come into agreement with His sovereign hand. Therefore, the words that He chooses to sovereignly accomplish typically pertain to the human race as a whole, rather than to personal prophecy. This does not remove His sovereign grace to intervene at any time in our lives, but keeps us actively pursuing Him.

Prophecy Has Timing

One of the first prophetic words that ever came over my life was "You will have an anointing to know God's times and seasons; you will move supernaturally in His timing." At the time, I had no idea what this word meant. However, if there has been one anointing that God has taught me in my life, it's this one—an anointing that many refer to as the Issachar Anointing (see 1 Chron. 12:32).

We must understand the seasons of God and not move out of His timing. In chapter 1, we talked about God's *now* times in our lives. Not every prophetic word is given in a *now* time. The

prophecy that Daniel uncovered for the children of Israel had to lie dormant for 70 years before its time came! Receiving a word about a future ministry might not mean that we should run off and move in that direction the next day. Such misplaced enthusiasm can cause us to move out of God's season and be less effective at what He has called us to do than if we had waited upon Him. It is like a baby who is born prematurely. The child may be alive, but he or she will have many more weaknesses, complications and developmental obstacles to overcome. The baby may never reach the potential that he or she would have had that child been carried to full term.

We need to be sensitive to God's development—of the training and mentoring through the circumstances in our lives—that will provide the fertile soil in which prophetic fulfillment will blossom to its fullest. By the same token, we need to know when to move with a prophetic word. When I first met Rebecca Sytsema, she was single. She had received promises from the Lord about her future husband, but she had not yet met him. In 1994, as several of us were preparing to go to a spiritual warfare conference, Rebecca had a dream that she was going to meet her husband at that conference. I immediately knew that this was correct.

When I got on the phone to make a hotel reservation for Rebecca, the receptionist told me that there were no rooms available. Without hesitation, I said to the hotel worker, "You must find her a room! Her husband is waiting for her there!" With no further explanation of what I meant by that statement, the people at the hotel were able to find her a room.

It was during that conference that Rebecca met Jack Sytsema. Two years later, I performed their wedding ceremony, and they have since had three children and are on a solid path toward all that God has for them in their lives. But what if Rebecca had not gone to the conference? I can't say that she would never have met

Jack, but she would have missed a now season and would have had to wait longer than God intended for her to move toward prophetic fulfillment.

This should give great encouragement to those waiting on a similar promise. God has the times and seasons worked out. Do not run ahead of God—but be prepared to move when the time comes!

The Dangers of Presumption

Another danger besides moving out of God's timing that we can encounter with personal prophecy is moving in presumption. In other words, we receive a prophecy and, rather than allowing the Lord to work it out in our lives, we presume to know exactly what the prophecy means and try to make it happen. The word may be accurate, but the interpretation can get us moving in the wrong direction. When Jesus was in the wilderness, Satan quoted Scripture and tried to get Him to act on it (see Luke 4:1-13). But Jesus overcame the spirit of presumption and defied Satan's attempts to get Him moving out of God's timing.

The enemy does not care which end of the continuum he uses to get us into unbelief. He can use doubt and hardness of heart to keep us from moving forward in the right season, or he can use presumption to get us to move forward out of season. When we move in presumption, we open up ourselves and our families to needless attacks from the enemy. We need to be careful not to presume when and how God intends to bring prophetic fulfillment. We must remember that we only see a part of the picture.

The way to avoid the pitfall of presumption is to obey the Lord in what you know you need to do next. In her book *The Voice of God*, Cindy Jacobs offers the following list of questions that can help us stay out of presumption when we are ready to make changes based on a word or a prophecy:

- Is this consistent with everything God has been saying about my life?
- How will this affect my current responsibilities? For example, will I be able to take care of my family financially? What kinds of stress will this put on my family? Are they willing to sacrifice what will be required if I make these changes in my life?
- Have I reached a maturity level in my life that will enable me to perform with integrity the new tasks and/or changes, or will I flake out because I am not properly prepared?
- Do brothers and sisters in the Lord witness to this word, especially those in authority over me?[5]

GOING TO WAR

Having given some basic issues that are important for us to understand when it comes to personal prophecy, let's now look at the spiritual warfare that is often necessary to see prophecy fulfilled. Just as God has a plan for your life, you can be just as sure that Satan also has a plan for your life. Satan considers it his job to thwart every plan and purpose that God has for you, your family and your territory. That is the very essence of spiritual warfare. Whose plan will prevail?

First Timothy 1:18-19 states, "Timothy, my son, I give you this instruction in keeping with the prophecies once made about you, so that by following them you may fight the good fight, holding on to faith and a good conscience. Some have rejected these and so have shipwrecked their faith" (*NIV*). Do you have a prophetic promise concerning your children, but they are not making wise choices? Do you have prophetic promises concerning ministry, finances, future direction, barrenness breaking off from your life, or any number of other

things? Keeping in mind all that we have discussed in this chapter concerning obedience, timing, presumption and prophetic evolution, ask the Lord if the enemy is at work to keep you from prophetic fulfillment. If so, it's time to go to war! As Jim Goll puts it, "Once you have secured an authentic prophetic promise, load it, take aim and shoot! Fight the fight and wage war with the prophetic."[6]

Praying a Prophetic Word

God's word has tremendous power. Remember that it was by His word alone that He created light: "Then God *said*, 'Let there be light'; and there was light" (Gen. 1:3, emphasis added). By His word alone He created day and night, earth and heavens, land and sea, vegetation and every living creature. Everything that has been created exists because of the word of God. Furthermore, as John 1 states, Jesus is the Word of God: "In the beginning was the Word, and the Word was with God, and the Word was God. And the Word became flesh and dwelt among us, and we beheld His glory, the glory as of the only begotten of the Father, full of grace and truth" (vv. 1,14). God's word, therefore, not only gives us our being but also provides our redemption and secures our future through Christ.

When God speaks a prophetic promise, there is power within the words. There is power to gain the supply we need. There is power to step into a new level of faith. And there is power to overthrow the enemy. Our own words also have a certain measure of power in them. Our words have the power to both bless and curse (see Jas. 3:9). Our words hold the power of life and death (see Prov. 18:21). And our words spoken in prayer can move the very hand of God and can block Satan's destructive maneuvers. Therefore, when we take a prophetic word that God has given us and speak it back to God in prayer, it is a potent combination. Jim Goll reminds us:

At times we must declare the [prophetic] word to our circumstances and any mountain of opposition standing in the way. We remind ourselves of the promise that lies ahead, and we remind the devil and command any foul spirits—for example, the spirit of discouragement—to back off, declaring what the written and spoken promises of God reveal. Each of us has purposes, promises and a destiny to find, fight for and fulfill. So take your "Thus saith the Lord" to battle with you and fight.[7]

What Are We Warring Against?

We can determine from the Word of God the following five areas in which we are in conflict:

1. **The devil.** Satan and his demons affect most of us. This includes Christians (see 1 Pet. 5:8). Satan has a hierarchy and a horde underneath him that are confederated to stop the purposes of God.

2. **The flesh.** The flesh tries to hang on for dear life instead of submitting to the power of the Cross and being crucified. Galatians 5:24 states that we should crucify our flesh each day. The flesh hinders us from obeying God. Without this daily crucifixion, we give the devil the right to tempt and ensnare us.

3. **Enemies.** Many times, evil spirits will embed in individuals or groups of individuals collectively and then use these individuals to set themselves against God's covenant plan in a person's life (see Eph. 6:12).

4. **The world.** The god of this world controls the world system (see 2 Cor. 4:4). Though we are not part of this world system, we still live in it. The world system has both a religious aspect as well as a governmental aspect that must be understood if we are going to successfully

maneuver in this world but never be a part of it.

5. **Death.** Death is our final enemy. Jesus overcame death, and we must war with the strategies of death until we have completed our life cycle in the earth (see 1 Cor. 15:26). And through His Spirit we can also overcome.

If we do not war against these things, we will never possess the inheritance that God has given us.

A War Strategy

Because of what we are warring against, we must have a war strategy for our life. In addition to the power of praying a prophetic word back to God, the Bible gives many other warfare strategies when it comes to prophetic fulfillment. One excellent example is in 2 Chronicles 20. In this story, a number of Judah's enemies came together to form a confederation against Judah and were planning to invade its God-ordained and God-promised boundaries. In obedience to the Lord, the people of Judah had not previously invaded those who were in the confederation and who were now arising to steal what rightfully belonged to Judah. There was no question that the combined strength of their enemies could have easily overthrown them.

Jehoshaphat, who was a godly king, cried out to the Lord for a strategy for the war they faced. As he addressed the people, Jehoshaphat said, "Believe in the LORD your God, and you shall be established; believe His prophets, and you shall prosper" (2 Chron. 20:20). He called the nation together and followed these steps:

1. **They fasted** (see v. 3). One of the greatest weapons we have in spiritual warfare is fasting. In *Possessing Your Inheritance*, Rebecca and I said, "Fasting is a discipline that most religions and cults understand because this sacrifice releases power. For the Christian, fasting is

essential. Often you cannot gain the revelation you need for your next step without it. . . . Fasting removes spiritual clutter and positions us to receive from God. By fasting, we make it possible for the Lord to more powerfully reveal Himself to us—not because He speaks more clearly when we fast, but because we can hear Him more clearly."[8]

2. **They inquired of the Lord** (see v. 4). This was a strategy David often used when he was about to be overthrown by his enemies. Each time David inquired of the Lord, he received strategic revelation that led to victory (see 1 Sam. 23:2,4; 30:8). Like David and the people of Judah, when we are at war and inquire of the Lord, we should expect Him to answer in a way that will provide strategy and direction for us.

3. **In faith they declared their God-given boundaries, reminding God of His promises of inheritance to them** (see 2 Chron. 20:7). As described above, the people of Judah prayed the prophecy back to God in faith. They let their faith arise. Faith is that pause between knowing what God's plan is and seeing it actually take place.[9] According to Jim Goll, "Take any promises that have been spoken to you by the Holy Spirit and turn them into persistent prayer, reminding God of His word. . . . Use these confirmed, authentic words from heaven to create faith within your heart. Let them pave the way for the entrance of ever-increasing faith in your life."[10]

4. **They acknowledged their own futility and recognized that they would be overtaken by the enemy if they didn't keep their eyes on God** (see v. 12). Even though we may feel powerless and helpless in the face of Satan's onslaughts, we need to remember that our

perspective is very different from God's. If we focus solely on our circumstances, Satan will use what we see with our eyes to bring discouragement and hopelessness, rob our joy, and cause us to be overtaken by fear. But when we keep our eyes on the Lord, we transcend our circumstances by quieting our hearts and minds and focusing on the Lord and His promises. Psalm 25:15 states, "My eyes are ever toward the LORD, for He shall pluck my feet out of the net."

5. **They positioned themselves to face the enemy** (see 2 Chron. 20:17). Positioning is a crucial element of any warfare. If we are not in position when the enemy comes, he will easily overtake us. We must therefore be sure that we are in full obedience to all the Lord has required of us and are walking on the path that He has set for us. Then, donning the full armor of God, we will be ready to face the enemy when he attacks. We need to ask ourselves, Are we standing where we need to be? Do we need to change course or direction to get into the right position?

6. **They sought counsel** (see v. 21). It is vitally important for us to surround ourselves with those who can give us wise counsel. Satan is such a master of deception that if we are standing alone, we can easily fall into deception. I have often heard Cindy Jacobs say, "If you don't think you can be deceived, then you already are!" If you are not under spiritual authority to those who are wise in the ways of God and are not routinely asking for their counsel, ask the Lord to bring you to that place before moving on in spiritual warfare.

7. **They worshiped and praised the Lord** (see v. 22). There is, perhaps, no stronger weapon of warfare than praise and worship to the Lord. Satan hates our

worship to God, for he is jealous of it and longs to obtain it for himself through whatever means he can. He also knows that the weapon of worship is strong and effective. Consider the words of Psalm 149:5-9:

> Let the saints be joyful in glory; let them sing aloud on their beds. Let the high praises of God be in their mouth, and a two-edged sword in their hand, to execute vengeance on the nations, and punishments on the peoples; to bind their kings with chains, and their nobles with fetters of iron; to execute on them the written judgment—this honor have all His saints. Praise the LORD!

Cindy Jacobs explains another important reason why Satan hates our worship: "When we praise God, He inhabits or enters our praises, and His power overwhelms the power of the enemy. He is a mighty God, and Satan cannot match His strength. Light will dispel the darkness through God's entering into our praise."[11] Through praise, the Lord Himself begins to do warfare on our behalf to silence our enemy.

The Victory

As the people of Judah earnestly sought the Lord and followed the strategy that He gave to them, the Scripture states that they were to stand still and allow the Lord to battle on their behalf (see 2 Chron. 20:17). In the end, it was the Lord who set ambushes against the enemy so that they were utterly destroyed. Verse 24 says that not one of their enemies escaped!

The Lord will do the same for us. We must seek the Lord, be obedient to His commands and let Him handle the rest for us.

"'Not by might nor by power, but by My Spirit,' says the LORD of hosts" (Zech. 4:6). If we are to have prophetic fulfillment in our lives, we have no choice but to believe that God will do what He said He will do!

The Spoils of War

This story does not end with the victory of the people of Judah against their enemies. There is something more that we need to grasp. The people of Judah's victory was not complete until they gathered the spoils of war. Second Chronicles 20:25 says, "When Jehoshaphat and his people came to take away their spoil, they found among them an abundance of valuables on the dead bodies, and precious jewelry, which they stripped off for themselves, more than they could carry away; and they were three days gathering the spoil because there was so much."

Can you imagine so many dead bodies covered in so much wealth that it took the people of Judah a full three days to collect it all—and it was more than they could carry away? God saw to it that their enemy was not only destroyed but also that the spoils of war were far beyond what they ever expected! God did the same for the children of Israel as they were being set free from their captivity in Egypt. Scripture says that the Egyptians loaded them up with articles of silver and gold and clothing after the Lord secured their freedom from slavery (see Exod. 12:35). Through the process of obeying God in warfare, *God gave them much more than was in the original promise.* He not only secured the boundaries He had set for them but also caused them to gain wealth in the process.

As the Lord brings us into victory, we need to ask Him what spoils of war He has for us to gather. What has the enemy been holding from us that he must now give up as a result of our victory? In some cases it may be literal wealth. In other cases it may be salvation for our loved ones. It could be restoration of destroyed relationships. It could be a physical healing or deliver-

ance from what has been tormenting us. No matter what spoils of war God has for us, we need to understand that the very nature of war means that the one who is defeated must relinquish something to the victor. Be sure that you have gathered all the spoils that the Lord has for you when you come into victory.

In addition to the wealth that the people of Judah gathered, the army of Judah was strengthened for future battles because they were able to gather swords, shields and other weapons of war from their fallen enemies. This represents a new strength and a new anointing that comes in victory. As we gain each victory in the war over prophetic fulfillment, God releases a new anointing of authority on us that gives us even greater power to overthrow our enemy in the battles that lie ahead.

> As we gain each victory in the war over prophetic fulfillment, God releases a new anointing of authority on us that gives us even greater power to overthrow our enemy in the battles that lie ahead.

A TIME TO WAR AND A TIME TO REST

Ecclesiastes 3:1,8 says, "To everything there is a season, a time for every purpose under heaven. A time of war!" When it is a time for war, we must have a paradigm for war! The church is being prepared to enter its most dynamic season of warfare, worship and harvest. When it is a time for war—*war!* David's greatest downfall during his reign came when it was time for him to go to war and he stayed at home. Passivity in a time of war is disastrous.

There are also times of rest. Not every season of our lives is meant to be marked by warfare. There is a time for everything, including rest. In fact, without seasons of rest, we will never be able to quiet our hearts long enough to hear the voice of the Lord or to gain revelation for how we should move forward. We need to be wise about how the Lord intends to bring prophetic fulfillment into our lives.

Yes, there will be times of war when we need to stand up and fight. However, the enemy will attempt to prolong our seasons of warfare in order to rob us of our strength. God's grace covers our natural lack of strength during seasons of war. But when He is ready to move us on, we are no longer covered by that same measure of grace. We must never get so caught up in our warfare that we take our eyes off of the Lord and fail to enter into the rest that He has for us so that we can continue moving forward.

Notes

1. Some of the material in this section has been adapted from Chuck D. Pierce and Rebecca Wagner Sytsema, *Receiving the Word of the Lord* (Colorado Springs, CO: Wagner Publications, 1999), pp. 24-25.
2. Graham Cooke, *Developing Your Prophetic Gifting* (Kent, England: Sovereign World, Ltd., 1994), p. 119.
3. Ibid., p. 120.
4. Ibid., p. 123.
5. Cindy Jacobs, *The Voice of God* (Ventura, CA: Regal Books, 1995), p. 85.
6. Jim W. Goll, *Kneeling on the Promises* (Grand Rapids, MI: Chosen Books, 1999), p. 172.
7. Ibid., p. 173.
8. Chuck D. Pierce and Rebecca Wagner Sytsema, *Possessing Your Inheritance* (Ventura, CA: Regal Books, 1999), pp. 134-135.
9. Ibid., p. 23.
10. Goll, *Kneeling on the Promises,* p. 173.
11. Cindy Jacobs, *Possessing the Gates of the Enemy* (Tarrytown, NY: Chosen Books, 1991), p. 178.

Hope Deferred

So shall My word be that goes forth from My mouth; it shall not return to Me void, but it shall accomplish what I please, and it shall prosper in the thing for which I sent it.

ISAIAH 55:11

Have you ever had a promise from God that you kept expecting to be fulfilled, but nothing ever happened? Have you had a desire that you felt God put in your heart that never materialized? Did you once have faith to see the plan of God for your life manifest, but now that faith seems dry and distant? Did you have *great expectations* for God moving on your behalf, but are still waiting?

Now we come to what is perhaps the most difficult aspect of prophetic fulfillment: hope deferred. When our hope is deferred, we can experience it in one of two ways. It can be either a promise that seems as though it will never be fulfilled, or it can be a

promise that is fulfilled, but the fruit of that promise is dead. Have you ever experienced the death of a promise? It can truly cause the heart to become sick (see Prov. 13:12).

ANOTHER DAY OF PROPHETIC FULFILLMENT

In chapter 1, I told the story of my daughter Rebekah's birth and what a great day of prophetic fulfillment that was. You will recall, however, that my wife, Pam, knew that the barrenness in her life would break off, because in 1980 the Lord had promised her that she would bear twins. As the barrenness broke, she gave birth to our beautiful daughter Rebekah, followed by our son John Mark. Then in 1987, she became pregnant again. However, this time, we noticed that she was getting larger more quickly than she had with the first two pregnancies. We learned that this was because she indeed was carrying twins! What God had promised was now in motion.

Pam carried the babies to term, and on February 6, 1988, she gave birth to two beautiful identical twin boys, whom we named Jesse David and Jacob Levi. God's promise had been fulfilled! But something was wrong in their new little bodies. One baby had a serious heart problem and the other had a serious liver problem. Within one week of their birth, both of our new sons had died. I watched as they were born, and I held them as they died. The grief and mourning were almost overwhelming. The promise of these twins had been the reason that we could believe the barrenness in our lives would be broken, and now, just as it was being fulfilled, that promise had died.

My coauthor, Rebecca Sytsema, had a similar experience. Shortly after she and her husband, Jack, were married, they inquired of the Lord as to the timing of having children. They received a clear prophetic word from a highly respected prophet

that the time had come. They confirmed the word and shortly thereafter conceived their first child. Within a few weeks of the due date, however, their baby daughter, Anna Jean, died in Rebecca's womb without warning or explanation. Their promise was stillborn.

How could this be? How could the Lord speak His promise so clearly, only to allow it to die?

SUBMITTING TO THE HAND OF GOD

When the second of our twins died, we had an outdoor memorial service for him. During that service, Pam stood up and sang a beautiful song out over the field. It was an incredible moment. One week after the death of the second baby, a friend called and said she had a real problem with the fact that God had allowed their deaths. She was also having a problem with how Pam was dealing with this trauma—with seemingly unshakable faith.

Pam told our friend, "If there's one thing I've learned in my life, it's that the quicker I submit to the hand of God, the quicker I can resist the devil. I have chosen to submit to God's hand in this circumstance. And in submitting to the hand of God, He will give me the ability to overcome the enemy so that the double portion that has been robbed will be returned."

The Lord was speaking through my beautiful wife. Those words went deeply into my spirit, and I have carried them ever since that time. Even when we don't understand what has happened in our lives, in the midst of our loss and resulting grief we need to learn to submit quickly to God's greater plan for our lives. If we always submit our lives to God, those incredibly hard things that we go through will truly become some sort of blessing in the hand of the Lord and will produce a greater prophetic fulfillment in our life.

ANOTHER PROMISE FULFILLED

In my case, the Lord turned the circumstances of the twins' deaths into a tremendous restoration for my whole family. My extended family, still distant in our relationships because of the crisis with my father that we had lived through, now rallied and bonded together in this new trauma. The Lord had spoken to me when I was 18 and given me a promise: "I will restore all that you have lost." These words had been the driving force of my life since that time.

Now in this terrible loss and trauma that Pam and I were experiencing, I was actually watching Him restore our family unit that had been so fragmented. My sister and I, who had struggled in our relationship, now were bonding. My mother, instead of being bitter and hardened as in the past, was now comforting us and walking with us through it all. An estranged uncle, whom I had not heard from since I was 16, called and responded to our situation. At 35 years of age, I was seeing God fulfill the promise that I had been walking in since I was 18. The death of one promise was the catalyst for bringing life and fulfillment to another promise. That is God's way. What happened in my family as a result of the loss of our twins was a true miracle!

LOSS HAS BENEFITS

We should allow God to work our situations for good and respond to His love no matter how difficult our circumstances may be. Pam and I both were able to recognize that even in this trauma that we were living in with the loss of two children, God was working out a higher-level promise of restoration on our behalf. Loss can produce a great acknowledgement of God within us if we submit to His hand. There are other benefits as well:

Loss produces shaking. During times of loss, God begins to shake us. He removes legalism, fear, condemnation, false expectations and erroneous ways of thinking about Himself. If we can endure the shaking, we come out in a much stronger place, which results in greater maturity. In the midst of loss, we have a unique opportunity to rise to new levels and come to a deeper understanding of God's awesome grace. His grace is always sufficient.

Loss produces joy. There are many Scriptures that link loss to joy. Stop and read Psalm 30. In fact, Pam and I put one such passage on the headstone of the twins' grave: "Therefore you now have sorrow; but I will see you again and your heart will rejoice, and your joy no one will take

> There is a certain level of joy that we would never come to know if we did not experience loss.

from you" (John 16:22). There is a certain level of joy that we would never come to know if we did not experience loss. The deeper the sorrow, the more capacity for joy we seem to have.

Loss produces change. After experiencing loss, nothing seems the same. Gerald Sittser, who lost his mother, wife and young daughter in a tragic car accident, writes:

> The experience of loss does not have to leave us with the memory of a painful event that stands alone, like a towering monument that dominates the landscape of our lives. Loss can also leave us with the memory of a wonderful story. It can function as a catalyst that pushes us in a new direction, like a closed road that forces us to turn around and find another way to our destination. Who knows what we will discover and see along the way?[1]

Loss produces resurrection. In *Possessing Your Inheritance*, Rebecca and I wrote:

> We can be assured that when we experience loss, especially of something that was part of our inheritance, God invariably has a plan for restoring it to us. When death comes, for example, God always longs to start a resurrection process. David W. Wiersby, in his book *Gone But Not Lost*, which was written to those grieving the death of a child, writes, "God's response to death is always life. That doesn't mean he gives another child when one dies. It means that out of the sorrow and ruin of your 'other' life, God gives you a new life." The same is true for any loss. God's response to loss is always restoration in some form.[2]

EXPECTATIONS GONE AND SELF PITY REMAINS!

We can easily lose sight of God's promises when we are in difficult situations. This is often how we get off target in seeing God fulfill our prophetic destiny. Even though the Body of Christ goes through great times of testing, we are not to grow fearful and be discouraged. The enemy takes advantage during our testing periods by using a strategy to discourage us. *Discouragement breeds hope deferred*, which makes the heart sick. When we have a measure of hopelessness within us, we lose our expectation of God.

"Future" and "expectation" are synonymous. Our future is linked with an expectation of God moving. This is a time for the Church to have its expectation level renewed and raised to another level. Isaiah 59 and 60 are wonderful prayer guides for us to follow to see this happen in our lives. Hope must transcend and move into faith. Faith produces overcoming. Overcoming

leads to a demonstration of God's power and a manifestation of His promises.

THE CYCLE OF SELF-PITY

Prophecy unlocks our future. But once we get wounded or experience loss, we can lose sight of our future. The biggest demonic force that we have to contend with is self-pity. Self-pity draws attention to our loss and keeps us from seeing God's glory manifested in our life. Instead of our loss directing us to God's continued perfect plan for our life, our self rises up and causes us to say, "Pity me for what I have lost." Any time we experience loss, trauma, wounding or injustice, we can either choose to live with a belief system that God can heal and forgive or we can allow our mind-set to form rejection, self-defense and self-pity.

During times of loss and wounding, we have a tendency to accuse God for the trauma that we are experiencing. The power of this accusation leads to a type of fatherlessness. Instead of experiencing the spirit of adoption, we feel abandoned and lost. From our self-defense, we actually form a rebellion to authority. We also become unteachable. We have a mind-set that says, "No one understands me or what I am going through."

We also begin to think that there is no solution to our problem. We wake up thinking, *There is no way out.* We fall into apathy because we have no hope of healing or restoration. Since we know that we should be living a godly life, religious mechanisms become a solace to us. We may even gain a martyr complex and say, "O woe is me. This is my cross to bear. Look how heavy is my cross." This type of thinking causes us to not fight when we need to fight. Instead of fighting and advancing, we become a slave to comfort and the status quo. We forget that we are called to fellowship with Christ's sufferings—a type of fellowship that leads to His resurrection power manifesting in us.

Losing sight of the love of God causes us to turn to self. God's love forces us to deal with these thoughts born of our self-pity. I have experienced enough freedom in my own life to know when I am not free. Faith works by love. Once we experience God's liberty and love, we will be able to resist that call from self to be pitied and be able to overthrow hope deferred.

JOSEPH: A PICTURE OF RESISTING AND OVERCOMING HOPE DEFERRED

I love to teach on Joseph. His story is one of my favorites in the Bible. Through Joseph, we can see how faith gives us the ability to see our losses come back to us in an increased and restored form.

When we first read about Joseph in Genesis 37, he is a young man with incredible favor and many prophetic promises. He shares these promises and revelations freely—perhaps too freely. Throughout Joseph's life, the garments that he wears are symbols of the favor with which God has graced his life. The famous "coat of many colors" that we read about in Genesis 37:3 represents both favor and a double-portion anointing from his father. But Joseph's garment is not secure. Even though God has an incredible plan for his life, Joseph will have to face many trials and losses before entering into his prophetic destiny.

The Betrayal of Brothers

In their jealousy over Joseph's favor, Joseph's brothers became enraged and literally tore his garment off of him. They sold Joseph into slavery and then reported to his father that he was dead (see Gen. 37:23). Joseph was betrayed by his brothers, and his favor was stripped from him. The betrayals that we experience in our lives are linked with covenant breaking. This is one heartbreaking form of hope deferred. When we have been betrayed, a covenant of some type has generally been breached,

which can cause us to fall into distrust and hopelessness.

When covenants are broken, it is typically the fruit of the covenant that the enemy will target. Divorce is perhaps the most prominent form of covenant breaking, and it is often said that the true victims are the children of the marriage. The enemy will attempt to use these kinds of events in our lives to not only strip our favor from us but also to cause God's plan for the generations that follow to become derailed through dysfunctional relationships and distrust in Him. But God can transcend these events and reposition us for prophetic fulfillment. Again, it is a matter of submitting to the hand of God.

We have to ask ourselves, Have past betrayals stopped us from having favor today? The moment these betrayals stop us, we can lose favor just because of our own bitterness. Joseph submitted to the Lord in the midst of his betrayal, and because of this, the Lord brought him into new favor with his master (see Gen. 39:4). Joseph had so much favor, in fact, that the master made Joseph his overseer and put all that he had under Joseph's control. God has ways, even in the midst of slavery, to bring favor and put us in strategic positions.

False Accusations

In the midst of Joseph's new position of favor, however, he suffered further loss through false accusation. The wife of Joseph's master became angry when Joseph refused to have an affair with her. During the encounter, as Joseph tried to flee the situation, his master's wife grabbed hold of his cloak and ripped it off his body. She then used the garment as false evidence to accuse Joseph of trying to rape her (see Gen. 39:11-18). Once again, Joseph was left naked, without favor and in shame.

False accusations can bring unwarranted shame and reproach into our lives and cause us to lose favor. This is why the devil loves to set up false accusations against us. We must remember,

however, that true humility does not receive false accusation. If we are not guilty of the accusation, sometimes God will require us to set the record straight and not just take it and think ourselves to be humble and somehow more spiritual. This is nothing more than a false sense of humility, which is a counterfeit of God's intentions. We may have to go into a hard prison over it for a season, but if we've been falsely accused, sooner or later God will set the record straight in our lives and get us back on track.

Lessons from Prison

After Joseph was falsely accused, he was sent to prison, where it seemed that he had been forgotten and abandoned. He had been rejected over and over and was now left to die in disgrace. Prophetic fulfillment seemed very unlikely by this point. The future, if there was one, seemed quite dim. Yet even in the midst of these adversities, Joseph did not allow his circumstances to stop him from moving into a new dimension of favor. Genesis 39:21 says that the Lord showed mercy on Joseph and gave him favor in the sight of the keeper of the prison.

We must not let fear remove our favor. We must not let grief remove our favor. We must not let betrayal, false accusations, imprisonment, unfair circumstances or rejection remove our favor. Even though Joseph was stripped, he continued to submit to the hand of God so that the Lord could clothe him once again.

Joseph also kept using his gifts. Often when we fall into self-pity, somewhere in the process we stop allowing our gifts to work. But when Joseph was in prison, he allowed the Lord to continue working through him by interpreting dreams. In the midst of adversity and hope deferred, Joseph did not stop moving forward in the plan that God had for his life. As a result, God found the perfect time to bring Joseph out of prison and once again clothe him with favor: "Then Pharaoh sent and called Joseph, and they brought him quickly out of the dungeon; and he shaved, changed

his clothing, and came to Pharaoh" (Gen. 41:14).

BUT GOD!

Just as God moved the heart of Pharaoh on behalf of Joseph, He can move anybody on your behalf. You may be waiting for a mate, for a promotion or for promises for your children. For these things to occur, God is going to have to move on somebody on your behalf. We need to have confidence that God will move on our behalf to accomplish His promises for our life.

One of the most faith-building phrases in the Bible is "but God." It is in these amazing words that we find hope for what lies ahead:

> My flesh and my heart fail; *but God* is the strength of my heart and my portion forever (Ps. 73:26, emphasis added).

> The nations will rush like the rushing of many waters; *but God* will rebuke them and they will flee far away, and be chased like the chaff of the mountains before the wind, like a rolling thing before the whirlwind (Isa. 17:13, emphasis added).

> For indeed he was sick almost unto death; *but God* had mercy on him, and not only on him but on me also, lest I should have sorrow upon sorrow (Phil. 2:27, emphasis added).

> *But God* demonstrates His own love toward us, in that while we were still sinners, Christ died for us (Rom. 5:8, emphasis added).

Joseph knew that *but God* had been at work in his life. In Genesis 45:8, he says, "So now it was not you who sent me here,

but God; and He has made me a father to Pharaoh, and lord of all his house, and a ruler throughout all the land of Egypt." Again in Genesis 50:20, he says, "But as for you, you meant evil against me; *but God* meant it for good, in order to bring it about as it is this day, to save many people alive."

Joseph knew that it was *but God* who had allowed him to be betrayed, go through false accusation, be abandoned, be rejected, and be imprisoned and forgotten. It was *but God* who had stripped him of his favor time and again. Yet in each instance, it was *but God* who had shown him mercy and reclothed him in favor. It was *but God* who had brought about the prophetic fulfillment and destiny that was meant to be his portion. For it was through this rejected, abandoned and accused prisoner that God saved the entire region from a devastating famine. Through Joseph, the promises that God made to Abraham concerning his family line were saved and restored. (We will discuss this more in the next chapter.)

Once you understand this, regardless of your circumstances and what you have been through that have caused your hope to be deferred and your heart to become sick, *but God* is still able to fulfill the promises He has for you. Once you embrace *but God* in your heart of hearts, you won't get bogged down under self-pity and defeat but instead will be able to say, "*But God* is at work in my life! I will not allow favor to be stripped from me, I will keep operating in the gifts He has given me, and I will move forward into my destiny because *but God* will make a way!" For those who are able to allow this kind of faith in God to arise, it is without a doubt that the best is yet ahead!

CASTING OFF OUR OLD GARMENTS

Just as the clothing that Joseph wore signified God's favor, in the same way the spiritual garment that we wear represents where we are. Our garment may be made up of the pain of losses and

hope deferred. We may be wearing a spirit of heaviness, as described in Isaiah 61. *But God* sent His son "to console those who mourn in Zion, to give them beauty for ashes, the oil of joy for mourning, the garment of praise for the spirit of heaviness; that they may be called trees of righteousness, the planting of the LORD, that He may be glorified" (Isa. 61:3).

It doesn't matter what the enemy has done to distort your identity in God. You can shake off the remnants of those tattered garments and be reclothed! After the loss of our twins, the doctors warned us not to have any more children, as they too might be born with the same defects. *But God* did not agree. Since that time, we have had two more beautiful, healthy boys. I can't say that it was all easy, especially the first year after that loss. *But God* has shown Himself faithful. He has restored. He has healed. He has moved us forward to new levels of prophetic fulfillment and continues to move us on an incredible journey of faith and joy.

Loss is simply a painful fact of life. Yet as we submit to the hand of *but God*, it can become a tool that propels us from a season of loss into a *now* season of joyous prophetic fulfillment. Declare each of the following over your life and allow your expectation of *but God* to be renewed:

- Expect the Lord to raise up a standard against your foes (see Isa. 59:19)!
- Expect your spirit to arise with glory so that oppression and depression break off of you (see Isa. 60:1)!
- Expect the Lord's presence to rest on you (see Isa. 60:2)!
- Expect new vision to arise within you (see Isa. 60:4)!
- Expect new joy to overwhelm you (see Isa. 60:5)!
- Expect that the "camels are coming" to your house with new supply (see Isa. 60:6-7)!
- Expect praise to begin to cover your region, breaking the power of desolation (see Isa. 60:6)!

- Expect God to release the strength and supply to complete your building project (see Isa. 60:9-10)!
- Expect new favor to come upon you and new doors and connections to open for you (see Isa. 60:10)!
- Expect the spirit of poverty that has been holding your gates shut to let go and the gate of provision to come open and stay open (see Isa. 60:11)!

Notes
1. Gerald L. Sittser, *A Grace Disguised* (Grand Rapids, MI: Zondervan Publishing, 1996), p. 130.
2. Chuck D. Pierce and Rebecca Wagner Sytsema, *Possessing Your Inheritance* (Ventura, CA: Regal Books, 1999), pp. 74-75.

Your Land Shall Rejoice: Prophetic Fulfillment in Generations and Territories

But when the time of the promise drew near which God had sworn to Abraham, the people grew and multiplied in Egypt.

ACTS 7:17

Joel 2:21-25,28-29 states, "Fear not, O land; be glad and rejoice, for the LORD has done marvelous things. . . . For the open pastures are springing up, and the tree bears its fruit; the fig tree and the vine yield their strength. Be glad then, you children of Zion, and rejoice in the LORD your God; for He has given you the former rain faithfully, and He will cause the rain to come down for you—the former rain, and the latter rain in the first month. The threshing floors shall be full of wheat, and the vats shall overflow

with new wine and oil. So I will restore to you the years that the swarming locust has eaten, the crawling locust, the consuming locust, and the chewing locust, My great army which I sent among you. And it shall come to pass afterward that I will pour out My Spirit on all flesh; your sons and your daughters shall prophesy, your old men shall dream dreams, your young men shall see visions. And also on My menservants and on My maidservants I will pour out My Spirit in those days." This prophecy from Joel reveals the heart of God to restore and bless His people.

GOD'S PLAN DEFERRED

In the last chapter, we talked about how our hope can be deferred. But did you ever stop to think about how God's plan can also be deferred? He may have plans and a destiny for us that we, through our choices, disobedience and sin, or through misdirection or other circumstances, never fulfill. When God sets the destiny for our lives, it is not just for our own benefit. Many others, and even whole territories, are meant to benefit from the Holy Spirit's work through us. Therefore, whenever we do not allow the Holy Spirit to carry out the work that He intended to do through us, He has to look for someone who will. God's plan is deferred for us as individuals, as is the work He is trying to accomplish in our families, our circles of influence, and our territories. However, this does not stop God from moving.

Joel was prophesying at a time of great devastation to the entire land of Judah. He was prophesying that there would come a "Church Age" when all people would call on the name of the Lord, be saved from their sins and understand God's kingdom purposes in the earth realm. The people of Judah had abandoned God's purposes. However, the prophet Joel began to see a time in the future when the Spirit of God would be poured out. Every person—young and old, male and female, slave and free—

would receive the opportunity to experience the Spirit of God. We find the account of this prophecy being fulfilled in Acts 2.

FOUR DIMENSIONS

What's the real issue here? First of all, even when we stray from God's purpose, He already has a plan in place for redemption. I call this restorative prophecy. God is working in four dimensions. We see this in the prophecy from Joel:

1. He is working to restore our lives *personally*—"I will restore to you . . ." (Joel 2:25).
2. He is working *corporately*—"Be glad then, you children of Zion . . ." (Joel 2:23).
3. He is working *territorially*—"Fear not, O land . . ." (Joel 2:21).
4. He is working *generationally*—"Your sons and your daughters shall . . ." (Joel 2:28).

Prophetic fulfillment is intricate. When God is speaking into our lives and has a destiny for us individually, that destiny also affects the corporate vision of which we are a part, the territory or land wherein we live or are assigned to, and the generations to come. When we don't fulfill the plan of God for our life, that lack of fulfillment affects the rest of the Body of Christ that our gift was intended to be aligned with, the city and nation of which we are a part or were assigned to, and the generations to come.

WAITING FOR THE NEXT GENERATION

In chapter 1, I told of the great potential my father had while he was alive. The choices he made, however, caused him to miss his destiny. The only legacy that he was able to leave was not what

he accomplished through his own obedience to God, but the hope that his children might accomplish their destinies.

To illustrate this, let's suppose, for example, that a dog is bred for the purpose of becoming a seeing-eye dog. She may come from the best line of seeing-eye dogs, may have the correct temperament, and may even show great potential early on. However, if the dog refuses to allow herself to submit to the rigorous training process, all the breeding and potential in the world will not change the fact that she will never become a seeing-eye dog. She may become a good companion dog and lead a life of comfort, but she will never accomplish what she could have if only she had allowed herself to be trained. Her usefulness as a seeing-eye dog lies only in the hopes that her pups in the generations she breeds will be able to do what she herself would not allow.

> Just as God has a plan for our lives as individuals, He also has plans for entire bloodlines that are passed on from generation to generation.

God's Plan for Generations

Just as God has a plan for our lives as individuals, He also has plans for entire bloodlines that are passed on from generation to generation. In our individualistic society this may be a little hard for us to grasp, but just as surely as our physical DNA is inherited from our families, our spiritual DNA is also inherited. The pages of genealogies in the Bible are there for a reason. The family line from which someone came was as important as who they were. Why? Because the promises and anointing of God are often passed down through families.

God's Covenant with Families

Over and over we read of God as the God of Abraham, Isaac and Jacob. It was from this line that the Jewish nation, God's chosen people, came into being. It was the result of a covenant. Many of the covenants that God made dealt with families, as the following represents:

- **Noahic Covenant.** After the Flood, God made a covenant with Noah and his family: "Then God spoke to Noah and to his sons with him, saying: 'And as for Me, behold, I establish My covenant with you and with your descendants after you'" (Gen. 9:8-9). Through Noah's family, God established a new beginning for the human race.

- **Abrahamic Covenant.** As we have already mentioned, God's covenant with Abraham had specific familial promises. In fact, Abraham, Isaac and Jacob, as the three fathers of the nation of Israel, were all partakers of the same covenant. As part of the covenant, God promised that through Abraham's family, all the families of the earth would be blessed (see Gen. 12:3).

- **Davidic Covenant.** The covenant that God made with David after the death of Saul established David's kingship. God promised David that his seed would rule over his kingdom forever (see 2 Sam. 7:12). It was, of course, into David's family line that Jesus was eventually born.

- **The New Covenant.** Through The New Covenant, all those who partake of the salvation of Christ are adopted into the family of God, with Jesus as the firstborn and a vast family of brothers and sisters. It is through God's own family that all of His work on Earth is carried out. He perfects His family bloodline. We find in

Romans 9:11 that He grafts us back into the Abrahamic blessing so that He can accomplish all in His people that has not yet been accomplished. Thank God for this spirit of adoption (see Rom. 8).

Family lines are indeed important to God. The family of which we are a part, whether by blood or through adoption, has both a godly inheritance and an evil inheritance that Satan has used to try to pervert God's plans, which Rebecca and I discuss in great detail in our book *Possessing Your Inheritance*. Prophetic fulfillment, therefore, cannot just be looked at individually but must also be viewed from a familial perspective.

PRESERVING LIFE

In the last chapter, we talked a great deal about Joseph and the prophetic fulfillment in his own life. But what did Joseph's obedience mean for his family and their prophetic fulfillment? Joseph was reconnected with his family in the midst of a great famine. Joseph, having been forewarned by God, was put in a place of authority to be sure that provisions were made for surviving the famine. As Joseph discussed this with his brothers, he said, "But now, do not therefore be grieved or angry with yourselves because you sold me here; for God sent me before you to preserve life. And God sent me before you to preserve a posterity for you in the earth, and to save your lives by a great deliverance" (Gen. 45:5,7).

I love the fact that Joseph realized his fulfilled vision even in all his trials and testing. Joseph was faithful to the vision and dream that God had given him. His life proves that vision restrains people from sin. Proverbs 29:18 states, "Where there is no revelation, the people cast off restraint." Without restraint of prophetic revelation or insight, a people stray from the path that

God has intended for them, go backward, and finally disintegrate.

God worked it out so that Joseph would be in a position to preserve the life of his family, the family to which God had made the Abrahamic Covenant. Preserving life is actually revival. It is taking what was once alive and thriving and breathing new life into it.

There will always be an awakening in God's people to preserve what God is trying to do in our families. We can be assured that prophetic fulfillment will come, because once there has been a promise made in your bloodline, God will activate it at some point to preserve that promise and bring it into fullness. Even if you are the first person in your bloodline to be saved, it is important to remember that when God created that bloodline, He had a destiny for it. Now, He is awakening that destiny through you. As in Joseph's case, it doesn't matter what you've been through. God is at work preserving life to bring His purposes about in your family.

PROPHETIC FULFILLMENT FROM GENERATION TO GENERATION

In order to help us more fully understand how prophetic fulfillment works from generation to generation, let's take a look at Abraham and see the six steps it took to pass the covenant promises onto Isaac so that Isaac could come into his prophetic fulfillment.

Step One: A persevering faith. Abraham had a covenant promise for his family, which included a son being born to him by his aging wife, Sarah. As the years of natural fertility dwindled and passed, Abraham had to stand firm and believe God for this promise. Even so, he maintained a persevering faith, and the promise through which the covenant would be passed was finally fulfilled when Isaac arrived.

As we have said before, God has a destiny for every bloodline. We need to come into agreement with what God is trying to do, even if we don't know the specifics of how it will work out. This requires a persevering faith that often overlooks the natural circumstances in favor of *but God*. As we allow that faith to arise within us, we will see the covenant promises of God over ourselves and our families begin to take shape as God causes the circumstances of our lives to come into alignment with His promises to us. Other examples in the Bible of individuals with such persevering faith include Daniel, who withstood the lions (see Dan. 6:22) and Caleb, who in his 80s advanced into his promise (see Josh. 14:10,13). What wonderful examples of faith.

Step Two: The covenant promise will always be tested. In Genesis 22, Abraham underwent a strong test. God called Abraham to take his precious son Isaac and lay him on an altar as a sacrifice. It must have taken a tremendous level of obedience on Abraham's part to make that choice and lay his son down to die. But Abraham understood that this was God's directive. He knew that somewhere in the midst of his obedience to God, God would have to settle the outcome and fulfill His covenant. The obedience was up to Abraham, and the rest was God's problem. Of course, we know that in the end Abraham was not required to follow through and kill Isaac, but even if he had, God would have had to find another way to fulfill His covenant.

The testing of our promises is an inevitable step in prophetic fulfillment. In fact, if we don't get past this step, our promises will not be fulfilled either for ourselves or for our families. Like Abraham, we need to understand that our role is obedience to God, and the rest is up to Him—period.

Step Three: Testing unveils provision. Once Abraham passed the test, God's provision came to him in the form of a ram caught by its horns in a thicket. Abraham was able to take the ram and offer it as a sacrifice to the Lord instead of his son Isaac.

In fact, Abraham named that place "The-LORD-Will-Provide" (Gen. 22:14) as a testimony to God supplying what was needed. As we pass the testing of our promises, God will reveal hidden provision for moving us forward. Things that we were not able to see before will become evident to us, and we will gain new strategies for continuing to move toward God's plan for our lives.

Step Four: Promises extend to new generations. Another result of Abraham passing the test was that God extended a new promise to him for the generations of his family to come. God said to Abraham, "By Myself I have sworn, says the LORD, because you have done this thing, and have not withheld your son, your only son—blessing I will bless you, and multiplying I will multiply your descendants as the stars of the heaven and as the sand which is on the seashore; and your descendants shall possess the gate of their enemies. In your seed all the nations of the earth shall be blessed, because you have obeyed My voice" (Gen. 22:16-18).

God is always looking for ways to connect His promises from one generation to another generation. We must acknowledge the generations and recognize that God has promises for the generations to come. Even those prodigals who seem so far away from God's plan for their lives always have some opportunity to return to that plan.

Step Five: Connecting to pass the mantle. Many times, we must participate in supernatural connecting so that the next generation receives the blessing from the previous generation and continues progressing in that blessing. In Genesis 24, Abraham came to an awakening that the promise he had been given, which had been extended to Isaac, could not be fulfilled if Isaac had no wife with whom he could have children of his own. Abraham, therefore, instructed his servant to find just the right wife for Isaac. Through Abraham's careful instructions, the servant found Rebekah, who became Isaac's wife.

What is it that we are to provide to the next generation for them to move on in God's covenant promise for them? Certainly a godly upbringing (Proverbs 22:6 states, "Train up a child in the way he should go, and when he is old he will not depart from it"), an understanding of who the next generation is in Christ, and lots of prayer top the list. But beyond good parenting, we need to gain instruction from the Lord regarding our role in assisting the next generation to reach prophetic fulfillment in their lives.

Step Six: Conception for the future. Isaac's gaining a wife was not enough in itself to ensure that God's promise would carry on. He and Rebekah had to conceive the next generation. There must be a conception in order to bring forth prophetic fulfillment. We must not stop until we are sure that we have conceived and brought to birth all that God asks of us.

God's covenant promise to Abraham also required obedience for prophetic fulfillment. Abraham was required to go through all of these steps and partner with God in faith and obedience, even in the face of years of discouragement. Through Abraham's faithfulness, all of the families of the earth truly have been blessed. What is it that God longs to accomplish through your family line, and what role do you play in your family's prophetic fulfillment?

THE ISSUE OF TERRITORY

There is another issue to be considered as we discuss prophetic fulfillment—God's destiny for a *territory*. A few years back, Bob Beckett brought a tremendous teaching on territories. In his book *Commitment to Conquer*, he writes:

> The human race is not the only object of God's affection. We are indeed the primary objects of His love here on

earth, but not the exclusive recipients . . . God also loves the land He has created. He cares about actual, physical soil and what comes forth from that soil . . . since the time of Adam, God has been busy distributing the peoples of the earth throughout the continents and islands He fashioned as their dwelling places. Indeed, He created every nation, province, territory and city for His own purposes.[1]

In fact, before God made any covenants with families, He made the Edenic Covenant with Adam. In this first interaction that God had with man, He commanded Adam to do several things concerning the land: subdue the earth, take dominion of it, and till the ground—he was to tend the Garden (see Gen. 2:15).

Planted in the Right Place

Places are very important in the Bible. Bob Beckett goes on to write:

> While the Bible mentions missions 12 times, borders and coasts are mentioned 96 times. Justification by faith is cited 70 times, while countries and nations are referred to 180 times. The virgin birth appears twice, while regions are mentions 15 times. Repentance is noted 110 times, while the earth is referenced 908 times. Baptism appears 80 times, while ground appears 188 times. Christ's return is mentioned 318 times, while land totals 1,717 times.[2]

Why are places so important? The reason is because while God has a destiny for individuals and families, the places where they live also have a destiny. In fact, the two are so closely linked that often we will not fulfill our destiny unless we are positioned in the right territory. Without the right people in a territory, the

destiny of the territory will not be fulfilled.

Jeremiah 32:41 states, "I will rejoice over them to do them good, and I will assuredly *plant* them in this land, with all My heart and with all My soul" (emphasis added). God carefully places us where we are to be. One of my favorite exhortations from Bob Beckett's book is the following:

> Even if there is somewhere else you long to be, ask your-self two questions:
> *"Who put you where you are?"*
> *"Why are you there?"*
> There can be only two answers to these questions: obedience or rebellion. You are in a place either because God put you there or because you put yourself there . . . If you are there out of rebellion, I have a word for you: Move, as fast as you can! Find out where God wants you and get there. Even if it feels as if you are being led out of Jerusalem into Babylon, remember that the Lord sees far beyond what you or I can see in our lives. Obedience to God always brings ultimate peace.
>   If you know God has placed you where you are, even if it seems like Babylon, I have a word for you: Stay there as long as God asks.[3]

This is a very important principle for us to understand. Our destiny cannot be separated from the destiny of the territory that we are called to. Acts 17:26 says that God predetermines the places we are to seek Him. When we are in that place, we are positioned to gain the strategy necessary to secure our portion.

Prophetic Fulfillment for Territories

As we have already mentioned, it is not only for our benefit that we must be planted in the right place. The more a territory can

come into its destiny, the more light of God's Spirit can be found in that place. The brighter that God's glorious light shines, the more Satan's darkness is dispelled. In such an atmosphere, we see greater levels of God's will being done, including souls being saved, people walking in their full gifting, and a general improvement in the quality of life. This is why spiritual warfare over territories is such an intense battle. Satan is dealt a great blow when territorial victories are won.

APOSTOLIC ALIGNMENT IS NECESSARY FOR PROPHETIC FULFILLMENT

God has a perfect governmental structure that produces transformation in the earth realm. He has a perfect order in His government that cannot be resisted by the desolation of our land.

Lands go into desolation when people transgress, sin, fall into idolatry and deviate from God's ultimate plan. Once this deviation occurs, demonic forces have the right to establish themselves in the land and hold territories captive. There are four main categories of defilement of the land: covenant breaking, idolatry, immorality and unjust bloodshed. When Joel wrote about the locust entering the land of Judah and devouring both the land and people, all these defilements had occurred.

God has a perfect order in His government that cannot be resisted by the desolation in our land.

However, we find that God has a perfect order in His kingdom to break defilement and bring prophetic fulfillment. When Jesus was ascending into heaven, Ephesians 4:11 says that He gave gifts to humankind. In

1 Corinthians 12, Paul shows how each member of the Body of Christ has an individual relationship with the Lord but is also corporately dependent upon each other in the Body. In other words, we can't fully come into our prophetic destiny unless we align our gift properly with other members of the Body. Paul then sets an order of alignment: "First apostles, second prophets, third teachers, after that miracles, then gifts of healings, helps, administration, varieties of tongues" (1 Cor. 12:28).

Our gift must work within the order that God has prescribed. Therefore, prophets, who are second in the order, must align their prophetic revelation with apostles, who are first in the order. This will produce prophetic fulfillment. The word "first" means "prototype" or "model." Therefore, what God is saying, prophesying or promising to us individually, corporately, territorially and generationally can only be modeled properly in this alignment. When our promises are aligned properly in God's divine governmental order, we will see the harvest of the promises in the field where we are planted.

CAPERNAUM: A BIBLICAL ANALYSIS OF TERRITORIAL TRANSFORMATION

When we analyze the cities that Jesus visited in the Bible, we discover a pattern. First, Jesus had a perfect time to visit each city. The people in each city then had the choice of recognizing Jesus and receiving His teaching and authority or rejecting Him. When Jesus visited a city, He not only affected the people, but also every institute of society within that city. His glory permeated the way they lived. His visitation brought changes to religious, economic, governmental (legal and military) and educational structures.

In Capernaum, Jesus first visited the synagogue and taught. Notice how Jesus dealt with the way that those in

Capernaum operated in the religious worship aspect of their society: "He taught them as one having authority, and not as the scribes" (Mark 1:22). Jesus used a *teaching* gift. This caused a demon, or unclean spirit, that had inhabited one of the men in the synagogue to cry out. Verse 27 says that all those in the synagogue were amazed and said, "What is this? What new doctrine is this? For with authority He commands even the unclean spirits, and they obey Him." This caused Jesus' fame to spread throughout the entire region. That is how transformation works.

In Mark 2, we find Jesus visiting Capernaum again and *preaching* the Word to them. Notice that this time, Jesus uses a different type of gift and a different method of transformation. He is also in a different setting—the home of an individual. Jesus then demonstrates a different type of power by forgiving the sins of a paralytic man. This completely rattles the scribes, for the religious reasoning of the time could not accept this as valid. Jesus asks them a question: "Which is easier, to say to the paralytic, 'Your sins are forgiven you,' or to say, 'Arise, take up your bed and walk'?" (Mark 2:9). Jesus had the prerogative to choose how He would transform the culture. As a result of this action, "all were amazed and glorified God" (Mark 2:12).

When Jesus comes to visit our city, we must respond. The glory of His visitation will either bring transformation or hardness of heart. Matthew 11:20,23-24 states, "Then He began to rebuke the cities in which most of His mighty works had been done, because they did not repent. 'And you, Capernaum, who are exalted to heaven, will be brought down to Hades; for if the mighty works which were done in you had been done in Sodom, it would have remained until this day. But I say to you that it shall be more tolerable for the land of Sodom in the day of judgment than for you.'"

When Jesus comes to your city, receive Him!

ALMOLONGA, GUATEMALA: A MODERN DAY STORY OF TRANSFORMATION

In his book *Revival! It Can Transform Your City*, Peter Wagner tells the following story of Almolonga, Guatemala:

> In the early 1970s Almolonga was a city of degradation in every way possible. Alcohol reigned, and drunkenness was endemic. Men would drink up their wages and go home to beat their wives and children. On Monday mornings the streets would be lined with drunks laid out like firewood. Sleeping around was expected behavior. Disease flourished, and the extreme poverty of the city had cut medical services to a minimum. Violence ran rampant. Children couldn't go to school. Overcrowded jails forced construction of new ones. Natural disasters seemed to be attracted to Almolonga. The land was barren, crops constantly failed, and food was always scarce. In Almolonga, people were born in misery, lived in misery, and died in misery.[4]

After describing a power encounter that changed the spiritual atmosphere of the city, Peter goes on to describe the same place today:

> God has been so highly glorified and exalted in that city of almost 20,000 that Satan is embarrassed and irate. . . . Some 90 percent of the people of Almolonga are born again. The largest and most prominent buildings throughout the hills surrounding the city are evangelical churches. . . . The city is clean. People are bright and cheerful. Well-dressed children attend school and their families stay intact. Of the city's 34 barrooms, 31 have closed. Disease and sickness, now rare, can be treated

with readily available medical help . . .

Poverty? It is a thing of the past in Almolonga. The farmers raise world-class vegetables, including cabbages the size of basketballs and carrots as large as a man's forearm. . . . The last jail in Almolonga closed nine years ago because there were no more criminals.[5]

TRANSFORMED TERRITORIES EQUAL TRANSFORMED LIVES

God longs for that kind of transformation in every territory! I long for that kind of change in my own city! As a territory comes into its destiny, the people of that territory are much more likely to come into their destiny. Territorial transformation is a key to personal prophetic fulfillment.

Almost every principle in this book applies just as much to territories as it does to individual's lives. Take a moment to glance through what you have already read in this book, but this time with your city in mind. Remember that the territory that God has called you to is linked in some way with your own prophetic fulfillment.

What is God's plan for your city? What is its "personality"? What prophetic words have been spoken over your territory? Even if you are not called to be a pastor or a leader within your city, you are a part of God's plan in that place. That is part of God's prophetic promise to you, and seeing your territory succeed is part of your prophetic fulfillment!

Notes

1. Bob Beckett, *Commitment to Conquer* (Grand Rapids, MI: Chosen Books, 1997), p. 48.
2. Ibid., p. 53.

3. Ibid., pp. 65-66, emphasis in original.

4. C. Peter Wagner, *Revival! It Can Transform Your City* (Colorado Springs, CO: Wagner Publications, 1999), pp. 54-55.

5. Ibid., pp. 54-56.

Understanding and Breaking Old Cycles:
Infirmity, Poverty and Religion— A Deadly Threefold Cord!

A "cycle" is an interval during which a recurring sequence of events happens. A cycle can also be a periodically repeated sequence of events, something that happens over and over at a certain time. A cycle can be linked with a time or an event and orchestrated supernaturally so that a repeating wound or injustice occurs from generation to generation. Satan loves to keep us going around the same mountain or held in a cyclical pattern. *But God* has a remedy for iniquity. By embracing the blood and redemptive sacrifice of the Lord Jesus Christ, we can break out of any old pattern.

Ecclesiastes 4:12 says, "A threefold cord is not quickly broken." The principle here is that when three strands come together, they form a triple-braided cord that is very difficult to break. The three demonic strongholds that we deal with most

of the time in our lives are *poverty, infirmity* and *religion*. Since any one of these can stop us from walking in victory, you can imagine the impact when all three of these demonic strongholds align with each other. This is why I believe that it is very important for us to understand how all three of these strongholds work.

INFIRMITY

Let's look at the first of the three cords: *infirmity*. Infirmity is a term that encompasses more than just sickness and disease; it is also related to suffering and sorrow. Matthew 8:16-17 states that Jesus "cast out the spirits with a word, and healed all who were sick, that it might be fulfilled which was spoken by Isaiah the prophet, saying: 'He Himself took our infirmities and bore our sicknesses'" (see also Isa. 53:4). Infirmity can also refer to a disability of one kind or another. Infirmity can occur as a result of moral or spiritual defects that cause our will to stray from God. Infirmity can be related to the influence of an evil spirit (see Luke 13:11).

Infirmity can also be linked to an overall weakness in our bodies or with anything that created the weakness, such as grief. Romans 15:1 states that those "who are strong ought to bear the weaknesses of those without strength" (*NASB*). This weakness is infirmity. Not only did Christ bear our weaknesses and infirmities, but we are also called to bear the weakness and infirmities of our brothers and sisters in the Lord. This is called intercession. Romans 8:26 says, "Likewise the Spirit also helpeth our infirmities: for we know not what we should pray for as we ought: but the Spirit itself maketh intercession for us with groanings which cannot be uttered" (*KJV*). We have been called to intercede for the sick, which allows us to bring before the Lord someone weaker than ourselves.

The Cycle of Infirmity

What caused me to write this book was an illness that occurred in my life in the year 2001. The manifestation of this sickness brought me to a place of desperation in which I sought God. The Lord, in His infinite grace, began to show me that I had a generational spirit of infirmity linked with trauma. The trauma of my past was continuing to hold this infirm spirit in place.

This was not the first time that I had ever been ill—illness and infirmity were a pattern in my life. As a child, I had been plagued with such illnesses as stomach ulcers, bronchial asthma and migraine headaches (to name just a few). From the time I became filled with the Spirit, I had learned how to resist the power of sickness. Yet I had never really overcome the power of infirmity in my life.

In the early 1990s, I received some bad reports concerning my esophagus and colon—they were damaged and creating a very dangerous situation in my life. The Lord took me through a series of bad diagnoses from doctors. Then, because of my internal situation, my body began to reject anything that entered it and to treat it as an allergen. I began to experience anaphylactic shocks. I was miserable, and at this point very concerned about my future.

At the National School of the Prophets that was being held in Baltimore, Maryland, Cindy Jacobs, a friend of mine, shared with me that she believed my sickness was related to the trauma I had experienced while growing up. She believed that my father's decaying leadership in our family and his premature death still held power over me. My first impression was, *How could this be? I have gone through so much deliverance. I have even written a book about overcoming the loss that had occurred in our family.*

I came home from Baltimore very ill and unable to digest any food. My brother, Keith, was teaching Sunday School and gave me a call after his class. He said, "While I was teaching my class,

the Lord told me that the sickness that you are experiencing is related to the loss of our dad." I thought to myself, *Why isn't my brother ever sick? My dad was his dad also.* So I asked him this question. He responded, "You had a different emotional tie with Daddy than I. His loss wounded and affected you in a way that it did not affect me."

Jesus came to heal our bodies; however, we find that His desire for us is to become whole in body, soul and spirit.

This was an eye-opening statement for me. I fell before the Lord and began to ask Him how to break this generational iniquity of infirmity that was linked with the trauma of loss that I had experienced in my life. Since that time, the Lord has led me on a journey of understanding how trauma affects our DNA and weakens our spirit. One verse that has become a life verse for me is Proverbs 18:14: "The spirit of a man will sustain him in sickness, but who can bear a broken spirit?" A broken spirit occurs when life's difficulties crush our abilities to resist. Jesus came to heal our bodies. However, we find that His desire for us is to become whole in body, soul and spirit.

The Effects of Generational Iniquity on Our DNA

People are often confused about how generational iniquity works. Rebecca and I explain this topic in detail in our book *Possessing Your Inheritance*, but I believe that a brief overview of this subject in the context of the cycle of infirmity might be helpful here.[1]

To fully understand generational iniquity, it is important to first understand how DNA makes the blueprint of our body. DNA causes traits from one generation to be passed on to the

next generation. As the cells in an embryo divide and multiply, they do so according to the structure of the base pairs in the DNA. The combination of these base pairs provides the hereditary instructions for how each cell will be coded in order to accomplish that cell's specific purpose. As cells continue to multiply, groups of cells come together to form tissues. Tissues, in turn, form organs. Blood cells are pumped through the body, providing oxygen to each organ to enable it to survive. The cells in our stomachs work together to digest food; the cells in our brains work together as we study and pursue knowledge.

When the sperm and egg unite and a new life is formed, already programmed into the makeup of that person is God's redemptive plan as well as the iniquitous inherited traits that will resist that plan from coming into fullness. In other words, our blood begins to war with itself from the time of conception. Since cells are dynamic, an iniquitous pattern in a cell's DNA can affect our entire physical and mental makeup. If something is passed on in our DNA that has been "twisted" or linked with iniquity, that message is multiplied wrongly in our beings.

The Spirit of God can come into our lives so that we can become sons of God (see Gal. 3:26). As we submit and yield our lives to the Spirit's work, He flows through our blood and cleanses our consciences from the thought processes linked with the iniquitous patterns in our bloodlines. Hebrews 9:14 states, "How much more, then, will the blood of Christ, who through the eternal Spirit offered himself unblemished to God, cleanse our consciences from acts that lead to death, so that we may serve the living God!" (*NIV*).

In my case, there was a generational weakness that had aligned itself with loss and trauma. *But God!* That morning, He showed me a generational iniquity that had occurred in my bloodline that was linked with my dad. I confessed this as sin and renounced the power of its effect. This set me on a new road

to health. I had four doctors who helped me greatly in developing a new order in my life. One was a chiropractor, one was a specialist in homeopathic medicine, one was a gastroenterologist, and one was my general medical doctor. Each doctor played his role in diagnosing my condition. However, it was the Spirit of God that had begun to change me greatly from the inside.

Jesus' Treatment of Disease Was Part of His Redemptive Plan of Freedom

Jesus healed sick people. This was one of His major ministries. He dealt with many organic causes of illness and individuals affected by madness, birth defects and infections. The blind, the deaf, the lame and others who suffered approached Him for help. I especially love the story of the woman with the spirit of infirmity who "pressed through" in Mark 5:25-34. She is an incredible example of personal overcoming. She overcame the religious structure of the day, the reproach of being a woman and the stigma of being unclean. She pressed through to touch the Lord. This caused the Lord to release "virtue" (*KJV*; "power" in the *NKJV*) from His own body that healed her condition.

In the Hebraic culture of the day, most people believed that illness was the direct consequence of sin (see John 9:1-3). However, Jesus shifted this concept by healing a blind man who had been sick since birth. When Jesus' disciples asked, "Who sinned, this man or his parents, that he was born blind?" Jesus answered that the sickness was not related to the man or his parents, "but that the works of God should be revealed in him" (John 9:3). Many wrong choices produce consequences that affect our body, but Jesus came to extend grace to bring us out from the bondage of the punishment of sin and into healing and wholeness. He had the power to both forgive sin and to heal (see Matt. 9:1-8; compare Mark 2:1-12; Luke 5:17-26).

On several occasions, Jesus used His own saliva as an ointment or anointing (see Mark 7:32-35; 8:22-25; John 9:6-7). I find this fascinating—one of the primary ways that DNA is collected for testing is through saliva samples. Jesus took His own saliva, placed it on the eyes of the blind and watched their eyes form. He also healed those who suffered from mental illnesses and epilepsy—sicknesses usually associated with demonic powers (see Mark 9:18). The Lord addressed issues of fever and dysentery (see Matt. 8:14-15). Sterility and barrenness were also major issues in biblical times. Regardless of the cause of their distress, people found that Jesus could truly help.

Why Do We Need Doctors?

As is the case today, *prevention* was the most important dynamic of combating disease in Biblical times. It is interesting to note that based on our current understanding of disease, many of the laws that the Lord established in biblical times would have actually aided in preventing and combating various illnesses. Diet is one of the most important facets of health, which is why we find a number a laws relating to diet (see Lev. 11). Wine was also used to help stop problems and alleviate pain and discomfort (see 1 Tim. 5:23). We also find the use of ointments and salves in biblical times that were used for healing (see Isa. 1:6). James instructed the combined use of oil, confession of faults and spiritual authority to produce healing (see Jas. 5:14).

In a world of chemical stimulation and overwhelming stress, it is a wonder that any of us remain healthy. Stress has such impact on our bodies—both physically and spiritually—that without the Lord as our strength, it would be impossible for us to live in this world. Jesus told us to be *in* the world, but not *of* it (see John 17:11,14). So why do we need doctors? One reason is because doctors are trained to understand dynamics *of* the world that can give us wisdom on how to be *in* the world.

Most doctors also understand cycles. If medical doctors begin to take a biblical approach toward an individual—that of seeing the individual made whole—they will be able to find the root cause of that person's problem and not only help to heal that individual, but also help to prevent disease in the future. With doctoral skill in prevention and advances in medicine, individuals can better reverse deficiencies that have created paths of decay. *Why do we need doctors?* Because they can validate what God is doing in a skeptical world.

One of my favorite books is *Dr. Gallagher's Guide to 21st Century Medicine: How to Get Off the Illness Treadmill and on to Optimum Health.* In this book, Dr. Gallagher says, "The body is a miraculous system equipped with an innate ability to achieve balance and health. We have, within each of us, the ability to work with, and nourish, this God given gift."[2] Dr. Gallagher suggests a healthier diet, nutritional and herbal supplements, identifying and eliminating hidden food allergies and chemical sensitivities, a simple detoxification program to get rid of harmful toxins the body, chiropractic manipulation, and following sensible health rules. He also gives instructions on how to break an old cycle, or "treadmill," which he defines as:

> Something that you run or walk on and get nowhere. An illness treadmill is something that snares you in an endless web of diagnoses, tests, prescriptions, and procedures and gets you nowhere, or even makes you sicker. . . . Once you are on the treadmill, you may get some temporary relief from symptoms. But all too often the cause of your problem is ignored, so things just get worse. Meanwhile, the treatments used to suppress the symptoms often cause side effects and new symptoms.[3]

Dr. Gallagher suggests finding the root of the illness and breaking the cycle. In his book he provides practical suggestions on how to deal with many diseases.

Breaking the Cycles of Infirmity

I have two friends from Oklahoma City, Dr. Dee Legako and Pat Legako, who are incredible ministers and also professionally trained in the medical field. Dr. Dee writes the following regarding breaking the cycle of infirmity:

> The practice of medicine very often involves cycles. It is frequently necessary to interrupt this cycle to effect change. This may be a short cycle, such as an acute bacterial illness treated by an antibiotic. It may be a longer cycle treated by a procedure. It may involve long cycles treated by changes in lifestyles. Whatever the problem (bad cycle), a tool is used to break that cycle and create a healthy (good cycle).
>
> Penicillin is an excellent example of treating a bacterial illness by breaking a cycle. The cell walls of bacteria are essential for their normal growth and development. Penicillin . . . cleaves to the –CO-N- bond of the B-lactam ring [in the cell wall], stopping the cell wall production, breaking the cycle of bacteria reproduction and halting the illness. Conversely, some organisms produce B-lactamases (penicillinases) and are resistant to some penicillins because the B-lactam ring is broken and the drug is inactivated.
>
> Colorectal cancer is the second leading cause of death due to malignancy in the United States. The vast majority of these cancers arise from [precancerous] polyps. Techniques are available to detect the development of these polyps (fecal occult blood tests, multi-

target DNA assay, flexible sigmoidoscopy, colonoscopy, double contrast barium enema and CT colonography). Once detected, these precancerous polyps can be removed. The cycle is broken and the cancer prevented.

Colorectal cancer exemplifies the necessity for continual maintenance. The known developmental and transformation process of these lesions lets us develop a follow-up strategy to prevent future malignant lesions. Depending on the initial findings, repeat studies may be performed at intervals from a few months to several years to insure that the malignancy (bad cycle) does not recur.

Diabetes mellitus is recognized as an emerging epidemic in the United States. This illness has many long-term cycles. Certain genes are strongly associated with the development of type-1 diabetes, thus the inherited cycle of diabetes. America's cycle of increasing obesity and decreasing physical activity is contributing to the development of diabetes. The human genome project and/or islet cell transplantation may lead to the breaking of the inheritable cycle of diabetes. Individuals recognizing their propensity to diabetes may break this cycle by losing weight, eating properly and increasing their physical activity.[4]

Dee's wife, Pat, a trained nurse, ministers to individuals in the field of deliverance. She writes the following:

Treating emotional and mental disorders, we see a number of cycles. These cycles manifest generationally and personally. The cycles can be broken by finding the root cause and dealing with it through deliverance, counseling, medication, or a combination of modalities.

Let's consider the diagnosis of depression. When we take a family history, depression is often seen cycling down family lines. Sometimes it is not recognized as depression. The person may be considered an alcoholic as he "drowns his sorrows" in alcohol, trying to counter the depression. The person in the next generation may not use alcohol but presents with depression as a diagnosis. The person in the third generation may abuse drugs (either prescription or street) trying to escape his depression. The problem in all three generations is depression, which must be recognized and addressed properly in order for the cycle to be broken.

Bipolar disorder causes cycles in the person's life. The person usually seeks help when he is in a depression cycle. This is followed by a period that we would call normal behavior. After this, a cycle of manic behavior occurs. At the onset of this cycle, the person usually is very productive and does not seek help until he cycles into a mania that produces a psychotic state. Initially this disorder usually cannot be treated with counseling and prayer only. Medication is often required to break the continuing cycle through the person's life.

Child and spousal abuse have certainly been proven generational. Statistically it is shown that if a person was abused as a child, he has a much greater likelihood of becoming an abuser as an adult. When a child is abused, he receives a spirit of rejection and often a familiar spirit of the victim/predator enters him. When he becomes an adult, those spirits influence his behavior, and he will abuse others. The way to break this cycle that goes from generation to generation is deliverance and counseling. Counseling alone is usually not effective, because his personality has developed with these spirits present. He

knows no other way of thinking or behaving and will be unable to learn new behavior until he is released from the demonic influence.

The Lord has been showing us how to research and write prayers for genetically based diseases. Schizophrenia is usually associated with changes to Chromosome 22q11. As the human genome project continues its research, we will be able to trace these cycles down generational lines and pray more effectively for illnesses such as schizophrenia. We are also researching how genetically based diseases are linked to generational iniquities.

In attention deficit disorder (ADD) and attention deficit hyperactivity disorder (ADHD), we see a generational cycle as well as a cycle of failure in the person's life. Because of an inability to focus and track a conversation, the individual does not respond properly. People with these disorders are labeled as slow learners, troublemakers, rude, and so forth. This opens them up to rejection and is a huge door for self-rejection. This cycle can be broken with medication and behavior modification. Once the person is on medication, the behavior usually is easily corrected because he or she can focus and participate in his or her treatment.

In any of these disorders, it important to seek the help of the Holy Spirit for wisdom in ministry. There are times when a person is in such a state of depression or agitation that he or she is unable to receive ministry until medication is administered. I have dealt with people who refused medication because they believed it meant they didn't have faith. I have talked with ministers who refused to minister deliverance to someone who was on medication because it was mind altering. If it is altering the mind to be able to think coherently and

focus, then they should be able to receive ministry. The good news is that there is help for people with emotional and mental problems. Look for the cycles and be prepared to break them.[5]

Whatever way you choose for healing as you follow God, find the root cause of your infirmity and press through into the healing process. During my time of infirmity, I had to make a choice to follow the Lord to Nigeria. Dr. Peter Wagner was leading a gathering there with key apostolic leaders from the nation. I always serve Peter whenever he requests me to be somewhere, but the thought of traveling to Nigeria in my condition was difficult to reconcile. Yet Peter encouraged me to go. He even said, "Because of how the power of God is moving there, perhaps you will get healed." He was right. I overcame my fear and went to Nigeria, and during a prayer meeting (of 10,000 people), the Spirit of God came. When communion was served, those who were sick were invited to come forward. I was the first in line. When I participated, I felt a curse of infirmity leave my body.

I cannot say that I have never been sick again. However, since that time, a power to resist sickness has become resident within me. When the power of infirmity comes against me, I submit to God, resist the devil and watch him flee.

POVERTY

The greatest spirit that we seem to be contending with in our material society is the second cord in the braid of captivity: *poverty*. Poverty is refusing to become what God has created and destined us to be and not believing that the Lord can branch us into the fullness of His plan. Poverty is not just experiencing lack but also the fear that we *will* lack. Poverty occurs when we conform our circumstances to the blueprint

that the world has surrounded us with. Poverty occurs when the god of this world surrounds and influences us with only a world perspective, causing us to forget God's ability in the midst of our circumstances. Poverty is the voice that says, "God is not able!"

Poverty can occur through various means. It can occur through oppression and wrong authoritative structures (see Isa. 5:8). It can occur if we develop a mentality of covetousness or gluttony (see Prov. 23:21) or are indolent or lazy (see Prov. 24:33-34). Haste leads to poverty (see Prov. 28:22), which occurs when we fall into "get rich quick" schemes. Poverty can occur if we resist the Holy Spirit and therefore negate the blessings of the Lord.

What Are the Causes of Poverty?

The main cause for poverty in our lives is failure to harvest. When we do not gather the harvest, a poverty mentality is set against us. Many times, the enemy will wait until our harvest time to develop strategies of devastation against us. Like the Midianites who always stole the harvest from the Israelites (see Judg. 6), the enemy has already devised a plan to eat up our assets and returns.

We can plant. We can watch our crops grow. We can even have a time of harvest. *But if we do not take our opportunity to gather and steward the harvest, a strategy of poverty will begin to develop against us.* When we increase without developing the storehouses to contain what we have harvested, the enemy will gain access to our excess and to our future.

Other causes of poverty include aligning with structures that cause interest rates to go beyond a godly mentality of interest (see Neh. 5:1-5), fear and an unwillingness to face our enemy (see Prov. 22:13), and (succumbing to) persecution of faith (see 2 Cor. 6 and 8).

Breaking the Spirit of Poverty

If the windows of heaven open, every spirit that has trapped us in the past will flee. One cycle that I feel we must break is linked to the spirit of poverty. We need a wind of change to blow upon us and produce victory!

Victory is the defeat of an enemy or opponent, success in a struggle against some difficulty or some obstacle that is impeding our path of success, and the state of having triumphed. We must declare victory over the spirit of poverty! This spirit has violated God's perfect order and produced instability in many individuals. I feel that the Lord is saying that we need to take a violent and passionate stand on behalf of the Body of Christ concerning this spirit—that we must press through difficulties and storms to force an atmospheric change. I declare that any atmosphere of poverty encircling around you or your sphere of authority will be invaded with the atmosphere of blessing and glory from heaven.

We need to take a violent and passionate stand on behalf of the Body of Christ concerning the spirit of poverty and press through difficulties and storms to force an atmospheric change.

The Church is in an incredible season of change, and I believe we are all sensing those changes in us and around us. I can hear the Lord saying to us, "What you seed will begin to produce great fruit." There is a grace for our offerings to multiply thirty- to a hundredfold. This is a season to gain victory through giving in order to break the curse of robbing God.

The Body of Christ needs to see restoration in our provision, for restoration is always linked with multiplication. Debt and

past financial defeats in our lives need to reverse. Any spirit of poverty that has held our generational bloodlines in captivity and kept us from the fullness of the prosperity that God has for us must be broken. The Lord is breaking the power of begging in His people. He is making us a people of faith. He will change the identity of His people from beggars to *kings!*

War to See Poverty Break!

If you are sent to war but lose the battle, you wear a reproach until you gain a subsequent victory. Many in the Body are afraid to war. But war is necessary in order to conquer our enemies and take possession of what has been promised to us. War is receiving grace to fight (see 1 Tim. 6:12; 2 Tim. 2:3-4). War is receiving the necessary armor for victory (see Eph. 6:11-17). War produces an opportunity for us to enter into victory (see Rev. 3:21).

The Lord used armies to bring His people out of Egypt (see Exod. 12:51) with a trumpet sound and a battle cry. He brought them out with the Ark, the presence of God (see 1 Sam. 4:5-6). He used forces of nature when necessary to help them defeat their enemies (see Josh. 10). God always releases strategies that enable us to plunder the enemies holdings, to prosper and to stand (see Matt. 10; Eph. 6). He has a banner of victory over us. While Jehovah Nissi puts a banner over us to cover us, the Lord Sabaoth sends the hosts of heaven to help us. He is God of the armies of Earth (see 1 Sam. 17:45) and God of the unseen armies of angels (see 1 Kings 22:19). *He is the Lord of the armies* (see Rom. 9:29)! He already has victory for you!

We are required to combat poverty by being kind and generous to others. Like Ruth in Boaz' field, we combat poverty by allowing people to glean in our vineyard and provide them with access to our excess (see Ruth 2). We combat poverty by developing strategies to help those who have been ravaged by systemic poverty. In other words, we help others gain wisdom on how to

break out of the system that Satan is using to hold them captive financially. We are also required to develop reaping strategies (see Amos 9:13). When we do this, we overcome and our increase will go from multiplication to multiplication.

May you be blessed and have success in all that you put your hands to! The Lord will give us the power to adapt to every circumstance so that we can have success and bring forth His covenant plan (see Deut. 8:18). To succeed means to follow after, dispossess the enemy and possess or occupy his territory. It means to master the place or position that the Lord assigns to us. Success occurs when we accomplish God's redemptive plan for our lives. If we receive revelation, honor the prophets and are at the right place at the right time doing the right thing, we will *succeed*.

Joshua 1:8 says, "This Book of the Law shall not depart from your mouth, but you shall meditate in it day and night, that you may observe to do according to all that is written in it. For then you will make your way prosperous, and then you will have good success." Success occurs when we behave wisely and act prudently and when we study to develop skill and understanding. There is already help on our road to cause us to succeed.

The Power to Get Wealth and Riches!

Wealth is an abundance of possessions or resources. During the times of the patriarchs, wealth was measured largely in livestock—sheep, goats, cattle, donkeys and camels. This was true of Abraham (see Gen. 13:2), Isaac (see Gen. 26:12-14) and Jacob (see Gen. 30:43; 32:5). People of the ancient world also measured wealth in terms of land, houses, servants, slaves and precious metals. The prime example was King Solomon, whose great wealth is described in 1 Kings 10:14-29.

It is important for us to remember that wealth comes from God! The prophet Amos thundered against the rich and prosperous inhabitants of Israel, who sold "the righteous for silver, and

the poor for a pair of sandals" (Amos 2:6). Their wealth was corrupt and under a curse because it was founded on exploitation of the poor. By contrast, "riches" means receiving the grace of the Holy Spirit to enable us to accomplish what we are called to accomplish. Riches are linked with accumulation, or what we have amassed. A stewardship plan is devised from our riches. The more we steward our riches properly, the more we will receive. This is not just a money issue! God is looking for people who will shift in their stewardship so that He can release a transference of wealth.

Give Your Way Out of Poverty

The issue of giving is probably one of the most controversial topics in the Body of Christ. Giving does not mean bringing a check or dollar to the church. Rather, giving is built around a covenant relationship that is linked around an altar of worship. Giving occurs when we recognize that *our King* is *righteous* and *legitimate*. We bless the Lord so that He will take His stand righteously on our behalf. Giving occurs when we worship! Giving occurs when we respond to authority with generosity and blessing. Giving occurs when we realize the lesser is blessed by the greater—that God is the Greater King and we should want to give all to Him. Giving occurs when we do not hold back what we have been entrusted with by the Lord!

RELIGION

The main reason why most people find it hard to give is because they are bound by the last of the threefold cords: the spirit of *religion*. In Matt 16:6, Jesus warns us to beware of the Pharisees. The Pharisees were religious—they even tithed—but they either did not know God or were unwilling to change when God was ready to do something new. The spirit of religion resists change. I believe that it is one of the strongest spirits to break.

One of the great joys of my life has been the opportunity to work alongside Dr. Peter Wagner, who has the best book on this subject, *The Spirit of Religion*. Nehemiah 8:10 says that "the joy of the LORD is your strength," and Peter is a man filled with joy. He enjoys people, his life, his family, his ministry and his own jokes. Peter never lets life get stale and rob him of joy.

One of the characteristics that Peter possesses, which I feel is a key to his life, is that *he loves to embrace change*. If God decides that it is time to bring change into the earth realm through new thought processes, Peter seems to be the first to raise his hand in the earth and say, "Use me!" Embracing change seems to be the key to keeping the spirit of religion confused.

I was pleased to accept Peter's invitation to write the forward to *The Spirit of Religion*. Being a prophet, I have had to learn how to war against religious spirits. In my foreword, I wrote the following:

> *What is a religious spirit and how does it work?* This book boldly explores and explains how this deceptive force has labored to stop the progress of the Church throughout the ages. Religion is not a bad thing when we adhere to the word's literal meaning: to consider divine things. The word "religion" has three meanings in the Word of God: outward religious acts, such as praying and going to church; the feeling of absolute dependence; and the observance of moral law as a divine institution. James 1:26-27 defines "religion" from the Christian point of view: "If anyone among you thinks he is religious, and does not bridle his tongue but deceives his own heart, this one's religion is useless. Pure and undefiled religion before God and the Father is this: to visit orphans and widows in their trouble, and to keep oneself unspotted from the world."

Religion is linked with worship. Religion, when pure, is very powerful. However, religion is also defined as an organized system of doctrine with an approved pattern of behavior. Behavior has to demonstrate a proper form of worship. This is where we move from pure and undefiled religion to ritual. Demons of doctrine rob individuals of their freedom to worship a holy God in purity by instituting rules and regulations for their worship.

I have always been a creative thinker and an expressive worshiper. I have been known throughout the Body of Christ as modern-day prophet who expresses the heart and mind of God, and I have always had to maneuver past spirits of religion that would resist this gift of God. Demons hate revelation from God. They resist those gifts in the Body that bring revelatory freedom to the members of the Body. They attempt to stone the revelation of apostles and prophets, because this revealed word establishes God's foundation in the Church for this age. First Corinthians 12:28 sets an order of governmental gifts in the Church for victory in the world. That order is "first apostles, second prophets." Religious spirits attempt to defy God's order.

Religious spirits can also just deny change! Our minds and processes of thought aid the Spirit of God to produce change in the earth, but the carnal mind is in enmity with God. Religious spirits attempt to block strategic thinking for the future. They can make individuals get so routinized, or in a rut, that they do not want to shift into today's methods for victory.

In the New Testament, the Lord's disciples had to have revelation of who He was, who they were and who their enemy was. The Pharisees had a choice either to

deny the divine nature of God's Son or to align themselves with Him. They had to choose either to keep rules in place that prevented any behavioral change in worship or to begin to worship in Spirit and truth. Most failed in making the choice that could have changed their lives, their families and their society. Therefore, in Matthew 16:18-19 we find Jesus taking the keys of the kingdom of heaven from the scribes and Pharisees and giving them to the future leaders who would defy religion and lead the Church into its future. The same is true today. We must know who Christ is, who we are and who our enemy is, and we must choose to follow the Spirit as He leads us into these days of transformation.

Romans 12:2 reads, "Do not be conformed to this world, but be transformed by the renewing of your mind, that you may prove what is that good and acceptable and perfect will of God." The word "transform" means to change, transfigure or experience a metamorphosis, such as a caterpillar, which is transformed into a butterfly. The Lord told His people, Israel, that they could change from being worms to being new, sharp instruments with teeth that would thresh the mountains (see Isa. 41:14-16). However, prior to giving this promise of transformation, the Lord says, "Fear not" (v. 14).[6]

Fear not change! Fear not embracing the paradigms that will bring change. Fear not confrontation. Fear not the next great move of the Spirit of God. Fear not letting go of worship methods in the Church that have caused us to become comfortable. Defy the spirits of religion around you and move with boldness into your future!

Infirmity, Poverty and Religion: A *Noose* that Produces Death

I love to study the life of David. One Scripture that has always intrigued me is 1 Samuel 20:3. In this passage, David says "there is but a step between me and death." David had to learn how to maneuver past the religious structure of King Saul and the evil power linked with that structure that was resisting change. Satan has a strategy of creating a shroud of death that blocks God's best for us. He loves to use religion to keep us bound in infirmity and poverty. This braided cord forms a noose that chokes out God's best covenant plan for our lives.

In John 10, Jesus states that Satan "does not come except to steal, and to kill, and to destroy." Our last enemy that we will war against is death. From a physical perspective, death is a term that denotes the extinction of vital functions—the power of death stifles its victim in such a way that revival and renewal are impossible. However, from a spiritual perspective, death is not the end of human existence but a change of place or conditions in which conscious existence continues. "The wages of sin is death" (Rom. 6:23). Death is the punishment of sin. But Jesus came to reveal the power of life over death. The work of the Cross abolished the power of death and removed its sting (see 1 Cor. 15:22).

We cannot fear death, for if we do, we will never be able to overcome the spirit of death. We must remember that because we are children of God who have been bought by the blood of Christ, we have the ability to neutralize the sting of death. So declare that you are willing to change! Watch your atmosphere become filled with God's presence. This is the year to break old cycles. Ask the Lord to empower you to break the old cycles in your life. Ask Him to tear apart the three-braided cord of infirmity, poverty and religion in your life. Ask the Lord to come

again and break you out of old cycles. Ask Him to allow you to experience His glory! Declare the best is yet ahead!

Notes

1. See Chuck D. Pierce and Rebecca Wagner Sytsema, *Possessing Your Inheritance* (Ventura, CA: Regal Books, 1999), pp. 178-182.
1. Martin P. Gallagher, M.S., D.C., *Dr. Gallagher's Guide to 21st Century Medicine: How to Get Off the Illness Treadmill and on to Optimum Health* (Greensburg, PA: Atlas Publishing Company, 1997), p. 7.
3. Ibid, p. 2.
4. Personal correspondence from R. Dee Legako, M.D., March 29, 2005.
5. Personal correspondence from Pat Legako, R.N., March 29, 2005.
6. Peter Wagner, *The Spirit of Religion* (Ventura, CA: Regal Books, 2005), pp. 5-7.

Believing for Our Children

Let us not become weary in doing good, for at the proper time we will reap a harvest if we do not give up.

GALATIANS 6:9, *NIV*

There are few things in life that can shake our faith and our world more than difficult circumstances in the lives of our children. Whether these difficult circumstances are caused by illnesses, rejection, poor choices our children have made or the like, we often tend to feel their pain more deeply than our own. We long for our children to experience success, prosperity, joy, fulfillment and a deep relationship with God. Most parents truly desire their children to have greater measures of abundant life

than they have experienced themselves. And we should! Children are an inheritance from the Lord. But getting them from tiny, helpless newborns to adults moving in God's destiny for their lives is perhaps one of the hardest and most demanding tasks that we will ever face. It takes great faith and great patience!

What Children Represent in Our Lives

Children fulfill a desire that is within us and represent a blessing from God. Whether our children were formed out of own loins or are our "spiritual children," the desire to multiply has been woven into our DNA from the beginning of time. This desire is part of the twofold blessing connected with creation and the covenant promise. God blessed Adam and Eve with the words, "Be fruitful and multiply; fill the earth and subdue it" (Gen. 1:28). The Lord blessed Abraham by saying, "I will make you a great nation; I will bless you and make your name great . . . to your descendants I will give this land" (Gen. 12:2,7). In Israelite culture, the conception and bearing of children was a matter of longing and great joy.

Children are valuable commodities and treasures that God has given to the earth and must be protected. In early biblical history, children were taken by creditors for collateral on debts contracted by their fathers (see 2 Kings 4:1; Neh. 5:5; Isa. 50:1). Today, the slave trade in children is rampant in the earth. Children are the greatest commodity of life in the earth—they are the future of the earth! This is why one generation must war for the generation that follows.

Children also provide a foundation for restoration. The Hebrew word for son, *ben*, and the Hebrew word for daughter, *bath*, both come from the root word *baanah*, which means "to build." Zechariah 1:16-17 states, "Thus says the LORD: 'I am

returning to Jerusalem with mercy; My house shall be built in it . . . and a surveyor's line shall be stretched out over Jerusalem . . . My cities shall again spread out [overflow with goodness] through prosperity.' The LORD will again comfort Zion, And will again choose Jerusalem." The LORD is stating in this prophecy that He will add sons and daughters to Jerusalem that will cause her to prosper. He is saying, "I will develop a generation that will cause restoration, comfort and transformation from your past losses." This is the purpose of children.

CHILDREN ARE LIKE PLANTS!

Psalm 128:3 states, "Your children shall be like olive plants all around your table." Some plants are fragile. Some are wild. Some refuse to grow no matter what you attempt to do with them. Other plants grow and flourish with little care. I think children are like plants.

My coauthor, Rebecca, and her husband, Jack, have faced unique challenges in raising the oldest of their three sons, Nicholas, who has full-syndrome autism. Rebecca recently attended a secular conference on autism in which the speaker painted a beautiful picture with her words. One year, the speaker stated, she planted a wild strawberry plant in her garden. Not knowing much about strawberries, she was surprised to see that her plant not only survived the winter but thrived and began to spread. In the years that followed, it grew with very little care and continued to spread. Finally, it took over her whole garden!

However, the same was not true of her orchid plant. This fragile and delicate little plant needed much more care. It required the right amount of light and water and the perfect level of temperature and humidity. The plant food had to be just so. The orchid's stock had to be propped up as it grew, and the plant had to be constantly checked to make sure that its grow-

ing conditions did not need to be adjusted this way or that. Unlike the strawberry plant that flourished on its own, the orchid needed constant attention to encourage growth. In the end, however, the orchid bloomed, rewarding her commitment with a rich and colorful bud unlike any other she had seen—one that she was indeed very proud of.

The strawberry plant describes many of our "easy" children who seem to grow, thrive and bloom almost on their own. The orchid, however, represents those types of children that we did not bargain for when we became parents. "Orchids" require a great deal of extra care, like the Sytsemas' son Nicholas. Without the right conditions of diet, intensive therapy, constant care and nurturing—in addition to copious amounts of spiritual warfare—Nicholas would not thrive. He would not learn. He would remain locked in a dark, lonely and confusing world of autism. With these types of children, nothing is simple or taken for granted.

THE IMPORTANCE OF PATIENCE

Whether our children are adults or are not yet even conceived, each of the principles spelled out in this book are an important part of believing for our children. In the same way that we would apply the principles of prophetic fulfillment, warring for a prophetic word, and dealing with hope deferred in our own lives, we need to stand and apply these principles to the lives of our offspring.

However, there is one principle that is equally as important as believing for our children. This principle is not only a fruit of the Spirit but also a tremendous component of faith. If we are to see our children move into their God-given destinies, we need to have *patience*.

Admittedly, waiting on God's timing is not always an easy thing to do—especially in a society such as ours that is inundated

with cell phones, microwaves, e-mail and instant this and instant that. We are conditioned to seeing things happen *now*. We want to stand on a table somewhere, shout at the devil, and see our children make miraculous, instant changes.

Sometimes God does work that way. But often, the way that God works seems to be more in line with a prophetic word that Jack and Rebecca once received regarding their son from prophet Bill Hamon: "I will heal him. But it will not be an overnight miracle. It will come day by day by My anointing!"

If we are to see our children move into their God-given destinies, we need to have patience.

Honestly, this was not the word that Jack and Rebecca were hoping for.

"Day by day" is a long, hard road that will wear us thin. It is so easy to look at our immediate circumstances and say that we cannot see God at work. The circumstances seem insurmountable and overwhelming, and often times it seems that nothing is happening. But if we are in covenant with God through Jesus and are living with Him as our Lord, we can be assured that God is very much at work in our circumstances to fulfill His promise of Romans 8:28: "And we know that in all things God works for the good of those who love him, who have been called according to his purpose." God is busily preparing for the orchids to bloom, and they will do so in His time.

Having day-by-day patience does not mean having day-by-day passivity! We must remain active in moving forward as God directs. We need to hear His voice, war with our prophetic words, remain watchful of the enemy's attacks, and always watch for the *now* season in our lives and in the lives of our children. Our patience should be active and full of faith and hope.

Not only should our patience be active and full of faith and hope, but we also need to be aware that there are certain things that God is working in us as we go through the waiting process of believing for our children. Patience—not only with God's timing, but also with our kids—can produce many worthwhile benefits in our lives. Here are some biblical by-products of waiting on God:

1. **Patience is linked with wisdom.** "A man's wisdom gives him patience; it is to his glory to overlook an offense" (Prov. 19:11). People with wisdom are people with patience. Proverbs 14:29 says, "A patient man has great understanding, but a quick-tempered man displays folly." The more patience we allow the Holy Spirit to work in us, the more wisdom we will have for living our lives. It is in the wisdom derived from patience that we gain the strategies to overthrow our enemies.

2. **Patience helps us persuade those in authority.** "Through patience a ruler can be persuaded" (Prov. 25:15). It isn't the fast-talking, high-gloss presentations that will ultimately persuade the ones who are in authority over us. Those who display patience not only know how to wait for the right timing, but they also leave a lasting impression of good character and dependability—a very persuasive combination. The favor of God rests upon those who wait for His timing. Just like Joseph, those who war in patience will one day rise up and come out of prison to stand in favor before "kings and rulers."

3. **Patience is necessary to possess inheritance.** "We do not want you to become lazy, but to imitate those who through faith and patience inherit what has

been promised" (Heb. 6:12). As with any inheritance, there is a right time to possess it. If we try to possess an inheritance that has been promised to us in a family situation before the right time, we stand the risk of becoming disinherited. God has given us promises for our future and for our children, but if we do not wait on His timing, we could lose the fruit of those promises. Hebrews 10:36 states it this way: "You need to persevere so that when you have done the will of God, you will receive what he has promised."

4. **Patience is a component of love.** "Love is patient, love is kind" (1 Cor. 13:4). This is a lesson that we as parents know better than anyone. Most of us seem to have a supernatural level of patience with our children (although it can certainly be tested at times!). With all that is demanded of us, however, we can easily lose sight of the fact that we need great patience in the other important relationships in our lives, such as with our spouses, extended family, and good friends. These are the people to whom God has connected us and who will fight with us for our children.

5. **Patience produces endurance.** "Being strengthened with all power according to his glorious might so that you may have great endurance and patience" (Col. 1:11). Marathon runners do not begin their training by running marathons. It takes the patience of training to gain the necessary endurance to run the race. It is no different with us. As we allow God to take us through the training of life, the patience we develop gives us not only the endurance to run the race to the end, but also the endurance to finish it well. "But those who wait on the LORD shall renew their strength; they shall mount up with wings like

eagles, they shall run and not be weary, they shall walk and not faint" (Isa. 40:31).

6. **Patience raises the level of other fruit of the Spirit.** "But the fruit of the Spirit is love, joy, peace, patience, kindness, goodness, faithfulness, gentleness and self-control" (Gal. 5:22-23). It seems to be a spiritual law that the fruit of the Spirit are interconnected. The more we have of one, the more we will have of the others. As we obtain more love, we will get more faithfulness; as we obtain more joy, we will get more peace, and so on. As we allow the Holy Spirit to work patience within us, we will see the levels of love, joy, peace, kindness, goodness, faithfulness, gentleness and self-control rise to an equivalent degree within us. The fruit of the Spirit in our lives will not only produce such benefits for us, but it will also undo the work of the enemy!

7. **Patience produces character and hope.** "Not only so, but we also rejoice in our sufferings, because we know that suffering produces perseverance; perseverance, character; and character, hope. And hope does not disappoint us, because God has poured out his love into our hearts by the Holy Spirit, whom he has given us" (Rom. 5:3-5). Patience is truly a virtue, and those who have it tend to have great character as well. But this verse in Romans indicates that those with patience also possess hope. Why? Because those who wait patiently on the Lord have seen Him move and know that He will move again. Their hope is in the Lord because, through patience, they have seen the depths of His grace, mercy and power to overcome any of life's obstacles. And they know that He will do it again!

No matter what our children face in their lives, believing for them will propel us into a new level of faith. It will test every bit of our beings, but in this area we need to remember that the best is truly ahead! May God grant you the patience in every circumstance of your life to see your orchids bloom.

GOD INTERVENES IN OUR WEARINESS

Pam and I have six wonderful children who we have been able to nurture here in the earth. Earlier, I wrote about the twins that Pam and I lost as infants and how we had to release and entrust them into the hands of the Lord. I believe that this is what all of us have to do with each one of our children.

Having six children of our own, Pam and I have become experts in raising our own variety of "orchids." I could write a book just on stories about my own children. Each one is unique, a bit on the edge, and a bit peculiar in his or her own right. Two of our children, Daniel and Joseph, came to us as a result of the Lord intervening supernaturally in our lives through adoption. We received Daniel before Pam was able to conceive children. He came to us as a newborn from our ministry connections. His birth mother was a Christian who had gone astray and found herself in the position of having another child, and she knew that she would not be able to take care of him. We had been longing for a child, and God chose Daniel for us. He has been a joy to me and his mother in every respect.

The other supernatural intervention in our lives was Joseph, who came to us at the age of 13 when we were serving as administrators of an institute in Texas for children from dysfunctional homes. (Actually, he came to us as "Billy," nicknamed after one of the men that his natural mother had aligned herself with, but we discovered that his real name was Joseph.) Joseph did not know his natural father, and his mother was in prison.

He was a street kid from Houston who had been in numerous foster homes and care group homes. As with many children who come from dysfunctional authority structures in the home, Joseph knew the "system" of how to lie and manipulate to gain favor. However, he did not know the Lord. He had been forced to be religious and to follow rules, but he had no reality of God in his life.

Our role was to lead Joseph to the Lord and fully establish him on the path that God had destined for him when He created him in the womb. We actually knew that we would have to go through a process to redevelop his identity and make him into the "Joseph" that God intended for him to be. He was a trial for us. Not only were we developing his character, but we were also undoing and unraveling many of the ungodly mind-sets of survival that he had developed. Satan had grabbed hold of Joseph's destiny at an early age and was attempting to hold him on a path of destruction.

But God! The promise that God gave me for Joseph was that he would be an "A" and "B" grade student. Oh, my! This was neither a reality nor a desire in his heart. War after war proceeded. He did make enough "C" grades to keep him in sport programs that he enjoyed. But the several severe strongholds caused by the abuses from his past remained and there was constant contention over these issues. Because Joseph knew "the system," our discernment level had to rise so that we could distinguish the truth from the lies in what he told us.

I would love to say that this was an easy war, but that would not be true. I came home one day after a discussion with one of his teachers at school at the end of my rope. I was ready to just let Joseph go down the path that he seemed to desire most. When I walked into the house, Pam turned from the kitchen window and said, "The Lord spoke to me and told me that He was going to fill Joseph with the Holy Spirit." My weariness and

unbelief took over and I said, "Oh great, that means I have to endure this war longer." Pam then said, "Well, you can agree with God or agree with what you see!" I chose to submit and trust the word that the Lord had spoken to my wife.

When I did this, two things occurred. First of all, I began to see that Pam had a dimension of faith that I did not have because of her mother's love for a son who had been given to her. Love and faith were working together to bring prophetic fulfillment. Second, I began to see how the enemy used weariness, turmoil, frustration and circumstance to cause me to forget the word of promise and plan of heaven. Remember, the only thing that the Lord had ever spoken to me about Joseph was that he would make "As" and "Bs" in school.

I would like to say things turned around immediately, but they did not! After high school, Joseph went to a private college in East Texas and then attended a junior college in North Texas for two years. Yet he was still mediocre at school and still filled with issues. Joseph decided to enter the Air Force, and Pam and I took assignments in New Mexico and Colorado Springs. Joseph married soon after, but his life continued to be up and down. I still wondered in my heart if he would ever really change. But Pam walked in faith and believed in God's promises.

When Joseph was 32, Pam and I moved back to Denton. By this time, Joseph had four children, and he was now attending the University of North Texas and working part-time. When he and his family came for Christmas at our home that year, he shared with me how they had little money because of his working part-time and attending school. However, he did have a special gift for me—it was his final grade report in college. He had gotten all "As"! He had made the dean's list and finished his schooling, just as the Lord had said in the beginning. He had finished strong! He had proven to the enemy, to himself and to me that what God had said about him was a reality. Both Joseph and

his wife now serve in pastoral ministry. The Lord had fulfilled the word He had spoken to my wife as well. I learned much through watching this orchid bloom!

DO NOT GROW WEARY!

Do not grow weary over your inheritance. Look at your kids as investments. Look at them as treasures that you have been asked to protect and keep from the enemy's hands. Look at your kids as God's training instruments in your life to increase your faith! Easy or hard, they are worth warring over! Remember, *the best is yet ahead*.

Avoiding Distractions

As we set our sights on the road before us and prepare for prophetic fulfillment, we need to be ready and properly clothed for the days ahead. We must not allow ourselves to be so diverted by our circumstances that we miss the Lord's plan for restoration and prophetic fulfillment. God has a redemptive plan for us. He is working all things together for our good.

However, distractions can often overwhelm us as we travel this path. In the previous chapter, we discussed how children can sometimes be one such distraction. Yet we need to remember that children are a blessing from the Lord. Children are not given to us to distract, confuse or overwhelm us, but to develop, mature and extend us into the future. One of my favorite verses comes from Haggai 2:9: "The glory of this latter temple shall be greater than the former." We need to always be mindful that God's plan is for our testimony to be stronger at the end of our journey than it was at the beginning.

Don't Get Distracted

I love the story of Jesus visiting the home of Mary and Martha (see Luke 10:38-42). When Jesus arrived and was welcomed into the house, Mary sat at His feet and listened to His word. She stayed focused on the highest purpose of the moment. Martha, on the other hand, became "distracted with much serving" (Luke 10:40). The word "distracted" in Greek is *perispao*, which means to be encumbered and dragged all around.

Martha even approached Jesus and said, "Lord, do you not care that my sister has left me to serve alone?" (v. 40). In other words, Martha was telling Jesus, "Make my sister come drag around in circles with me!" But Jesus responded, "Martha, Martha, you are worried and troubled about many things. But one thing is needed, and Mary has chosen that good part, which will not be taken away from her" (vv. 41-42).

This is a time in history when the events occurring around us can distract us from the highest purpose of God. With so much to deal with in our daily lives and with all the cares of the world, it is easy to become "worried and troubled about many things." In the Greek, the word for "worry" is *merimnao*, which means "to divide in parts." This word can also suggest a distraction or a preoccupation with things causing anxiety, stress and pressure. It means straying from a focused goal that we are called to accomplish. In Matthew 6:25-30, Jesus states:

> Therefore I say to you, do not worry about your life, what you will eat or what you will drink; nor about your body, what you will put on. Is not life more than food and the body more than clothing? Look at the birds of the air . . . Are you not of more value than they? . . . So why do you worry about clothing? Consider the lilies of the field, how they grow: they neither toil nor spin;

and yet I say to you that even Solomon in all his glory was not arrayed like one of these. Now if God so clothes the grass of the field, which today is, and tomorrow is thrown into the oven, will He not much more clothe you, O you of little faith?

Distraction and worry can fragment us. Martha was proud of her home and glad to have the Lord visiting, but she missed the purpose of His visit. Jesus was not there on a social visit. He was there to release His word to the city of Bethany. Mary's focus and attention enabled her to be able to perceive the best that was yet ahead for her life. Martha's distraction put her in danger of missing the best that God had for her. She became distracted and preoccupied instead of taking the opportunity to gain necessary revelation for her future.

We must work when God says work, but we need to be intimate when we have the opportunity to be intimate. Whatever we are doing, we must always stay focused and avoid becoming distracted.

LAZARUS, COME FORTH!

Let's continue to follow the story of Mary's and Martha's relationship with Jesus. In John 11, Mary and Martha encounter a terrible crisis when their brother, Lazarus, becomes ill. They have seen Jesus' power in the past, so they ask Him to come visit Lazarus, saying, "Lord, behold, he whom You love is sick" (v. 3) Jesus sends back a reply and says, "This sickness is not unto death, but for the glory of God" (v. 4).

This is a wonderful story in John 11. I love verse 5: "Now Jesus loved Martha and her sister and Lazarus." However, "When [Jesus] heard that he was sick, He stayed two more days in the place where He was" (v. 6). So many times when we are in terri-

ble circumstances in our lives, we forget the Lord's love for us. Other times when we are asking Him to fulfill a desire of our heart and He says, "Wait," we lose sight of His faithfulness to us. From this story of Lazarus, we can learn many things:

Jesus could not be coerced out of the Father's timing. Jesus watched for key *opportune times* to reflect the Father's glory from heaven. Even though Jesus loved Lazarus, Mary and Martha, He did not immediately leave His post to visit His sick friend. Instead, He waited two days.

In those days, it was believed that the soul hovered near the deceased for three days and then returned to God. Jesus' delay meant that Lazarus was in the grave for *four* days. According to the beliefs of the time, this meant that Lazarus was good and dead and that his soul had departed. In fact, this is the only record in the Bible of a resurrection occurring past three days.

This event revealed Jesus' ability to control His emotion. Even friends and close acquaintances could not coerce Him out of the Father's timing. He was not moved to action by external forces. This is a key principle for us to remember in the days ahead. We must control our emotions to keep us in God's perfect timing and ensure that we will be at the right place at the right time.

Jesus chose the key place to address the strongman of unbelief. In John 11:7, Jesus told His disciples that it was now time to visit Lazarus at the house of Mary and Martha in Bethany. Bethany was a gateway into Judea, a stronghold of religion and unbelief.

We need to look for those key gateways in the regions where we live. Unbelief is such a hindering force that it will keep us from seeing the best that God has for us in days ahead. Yet it was in this same atmosphere that Jesus preformed this powerful miracle of raising Lazarus from the dead.

Jesus revealed the progression of faith that is necessary to overcome. Jesus kept working with Martha, Mary and His

disciples to show them His character. He encouraged them to believe. "If you will believe . . . " Jesus kept saying, "You will see the glory of God" (see John 11:15,26,40). Our faith level must be raised to a new dimension in the Body of Christ to overcome what is ahead. Resurrection, life and faith have a proportionate relationship, which is necessary for us to understand if we are to overcome what is ahead in our future.

Jesus turned hopelessness into resurrection power. Martha and Mary had lost all hope of seeing their brother again. However, Jesus kept breaking the power of hopelessness and encouraging them in faith. We must be delivered from hope deferred now!

To resurrect means to bring to view, to attention, or to use again; to raise from the dead; to raise again to life. Why did John devote so much time to this particular miracle? Was the raising of a dead person the issue? What was the relationship of this particular display of power and the events that were to come? Jesus stated that Lazarus's sickness was not unto death, but for the glory of God. This was a culminating event in Jesus' life that eventually led to His own death and to the ultimate defeat of the dark powers holding humanity. Jesus overcame and was resurrected and, in doing so, defeated hopelessness in our lives.

Jesus' display of power produced relationships or brought division. Jesus' display of power in raising Lazarus from the dead caused individuals to either choose to begin to plot His death or to shout "Hosanna" and usher Him in as King. The Body of Christ is about to be realigned over the display of the power of God. But don't expect everyone to receive the power that will be displayed in the days ahead. The power of God is life to many but is death to others.

Jesus' shout of "come forth!" created a recovery. When Jesus shouted, "Come forth!" Lazarus was brought back to life (see John 11:43). This is a season of recovery in the Body of Christ. Hear the Lord shouting over you, *"Come forth!"* This means "to

escape, break out, bring forth, draw to an end, lead out, or to depart from a condemned situation." *Come forth!* Let this shout of the Lord rise in your midst and declare a recovery of what you have lost in the past season. Below is a list of areas for you to proclaim this supernatural recovery in your life, along with Scripture for you to declare victory in these areas:

- Recover lost and broken relationships (Gen. 45)
- Recover your prophetic call (Ps. 105:19)
- Recover delayed promises (2 Cor. 1:20)
- Recover the spirit and gift of faith (Rom. 1:17; Ps. 23:3)
- Recover the miracle of healing (Jer. 30:17)
- Recover your spiritual stability (Mal. 3:10; Ps. 129:8)
- Recover your financial stability (1 Sam. 7:11-14; 2 Chron. 20:6)
- Recover joy (Neh. 8:10)
- Recover wasted years (Joel 2:25)
- Recover the lost sheep stolen from your pasture (1 Sam. 17:34-37; 30:20)
- Recover the blessings of God (Prov. 3:32; Deut. 28:1-4)
- Recover all (1 Sam. 30:8)

GOD IS ABLE!

I awakened one morning with the following words flowing through my spirit: *"God is able!"* The Holy Spirit seemed to be beckoning me to pray for God's people. In my prayers, I was to declare *God's ability to make each one of us able to overcome.* I saw that we as God's people were hearing the Lord, but that our hearing was not turning into the necessary faith to overcome. I asked the Lord what the problem was, and He said the following: *"My people are to go from faith in one situation to faith in the next. They are struggling in their going. They have weak faith. They are*

allowing circumstances to sidetrack their expectations and hopes of Me performing future happenings that will produce favorable outcomes in their lives. These circumstances are keeping them from entering into *My* creative power. This new vigor and strength that I can release will catapult them into this next dimension. *I am able. Lean not on your own abilities, for I can enable you.*"

Faith should be growing and steadfast. Faith should be abiding and continuing. Faith should be producing work in God's kingdom. We have grown anxious in the cares of this world. We have fallen into fear of failure, fear of harm, fear of abandonment and fear of the future. We have forgotten God's ability to bless.

God is able to make us endure until we get to our "there"! When you endure, it is as if you repair a broken foot so that you can step forward, continue on your journey and possess the promise that God has for you. I declare that anything that has caused your "feet" to have broken peace in your spiritual walk will be mended and that you will continue on your journey to prophetic fulfillment. "And God is able to make all grace abound toward you, that you, always having all sufficiency in all things, may have an abundance for every good work" (2 Cor. 9:8). Receive God's superabundant grace so that every hindrance in your path that is keeping you from reaching your "there" will be overcome and your life cycle will be fulfilled.

> Receive God's superabundant grace so that every hindrance in your path that is keeping you from reaching your "there" will be overcome and your life cycle will be fulfilled.

A TIME FOR *WAR!*

War occurs when we engage in the conflict against our enemy. War is receiving the grace to fight. We war with our prophetic word! We win the war when our prophetic word from the Lord is skillfully used to dissect the enemy's plans. Yet when we read about "a time of war" in Ecclesiastes 3:1-8, I am not sure any of us get excited.

In his book *The Way of a Warrior,* Harry Jackson states:

> Spiritual war, like natural war, is waged with strategic goals on many fronts. Control of the skies, for example, is essential in modern warfare. As Christians think about air control, we could equate this critical dimension of war to the power of prayer. Although Satan is the prince of the power of the air (Eph. 2:2), we can defeat his forces by focused, persistent prayer. Our land strategies, on the other hand, have to include occupying or transforming critical posts in politics and law, plus positions in the arts, entertainment, fashion, sports, education, business and the organized Church. . . . The Church's ground battle must focus on raising up leaders who cannot be tempted to misuse their authority.[1]

Understanding timing and gaining strategy is a key to winning the spiritual war around you. War in the heavens and earth will continue to intensify as the Lord's coming gets nearer and nearer. Although this war is not with flesh and blood per se, it does manifest in flesh and war. The spiritual war will manifest in the earth in those who are against God's covenant plan. The spirit of antichrist will oppose the Spirit of the Lord in those walking in the earth. However, the word of the Lord is that the best is yet ahead!

A Seven Year War Season

I always try to go by the Hebraic calendar, because that is how the word of God was revealed. In September 2001, we entered the Hebrew Year 5762. Of course, most of us remember the beginning of this year by the World Trade Center event in New York City. However, what this year actually meant was that we were entering into a "Seven Year War Season." Rebecca and I wrote *The Future War of the Church* prior to September 2001 to help the Body shift into a mind-set for war.[2] This book is still very helpful today. Much of what was written to prepare us for war is now an actuality in our daily lives.

In October 2000, I was in a state meeting in Oklahoma and heard the Lord speak the following: "I have keys in My hand. I am reviewing authority from city to city, state to state, and region to region . . . War will now break out in these next 18 months. This will be a war of great spiritual magnitude. The war will be over the boundaries of the future—for the enemy has shifted boundaries."

In that same meeting, the Lord also said:

I am setting My course for judgment upon the states of this land. I will be judging the states of this land, and judgment will be evident by February 2002. Judgment will come based upon the complacency of the church from state to state. For you have thought judgment would come based upon the civil government that is in place, but I would say to you that judgment will come because of the complacency of My people. . . .

It is important *now* how you motivate those around you to respond to Me. For it is based upon the response of My people now that I will determine those who go into drought and those who go into natural disaster. I say to

you also, *I will release judgment from state to state based upon the response that I see concerning My Spirit dwelling on this earth.* . . . For I say it is My Spirit that is the restraining force in this land, and based upon how My Spirit is welcomed in a territory is how I will begin to allow demonic forces to rise up and how I will begin to dethrone demonic forces. . . .

So I say to you, do not be a people who operate in false judgment, for My judgment will come only based upon complacency and My judgment will only come upon the welcoming of My Spirit into your territories. . . . This will be a time of determining the authority at the gates of your cities and states. The rulership of the gates is being determined *now.* . . .

There is a war over the justice of this land. I will establish justice in the midst of My people; therefore, there will be war over laws that have been established wrongly. . . . Know that you are warring with an antichrist system. Therefore, do not fear this supernatural war that I am calling My people to be engaged in. Align yourself properly for war.

I knew that we had entered a key *kairos* (opportune) time. This word generated in me a burden for our nation for this particular season. In *God's Timing for Your Life,* Dutch Sheets says:

At the Pool of Bethesda, Jesus came to the man who had been in his paralyzed condition for 36 years and asked him what seemed to be a strange question: "Do you want to get well?" (John 5:6, *NIV*). The man's answer revealed that although he was waiting at the pool, he really had no hope of being healed. He was in a kairos moment, close to fullness, but hopelessness had set in. Jesus asked

him this question to make him realize that, although he was waiting for the miraculous stirring in the pool, he had lost all hope of actually being healed. Only seconds away from experiencing the new, just a handclasp away from total restoration, the man was too disillusioned to recognize it. Somewhere along the way, as he went through the process of time, he lost his expectation. There wasn't anything within him that could respond in hope to Jesus' question. When God brings a shift, we must be ready to shift with Him. If we're not careful, we won't believe that He can bring us from the chronos stages through the kairos seasons and into fullness.[3]

In January 2001, I continued to hear the Lord say, "There will be a *restoration* of the *war mantle* of the Body of Christ." The Lord then revealed to me that we would actually be at war in the United States by September 18 of that year. This statement produced quite a bit of controversy. As Americans, we could not wrap our minds around the concept of war coming to the United States because we were living in peace and prosperity. However, the statement proved to be a truth that God was communicating from heaven to the earth realm in order to prepare His people for the future.

Notes

1. Harry R. Jackson, *The Way of a Warrior: How to Fulfill Life's Most Difficult Assignments* (Grand Rapids, MI: Chosen Books, 2005), pp. 21-22.
2. Chuck Pierce and Rebecca Sytsema, *The Future War of the Church* (Ventura, CA: Regal Books, 2001).
3. Dutch Sheets, *God's Timing for Your Life* (Ventura, CA: Regal Books, 2001), p. 33.

Ready and Clothed for the Best Ahead:

A Call To Advance!

September 11, 2001, was a defining day for the world. We all stood in horror as we watched the World Trade Center crumble before our eyes as a result of the terrorist attacks upon America. Simultaneously, the Pentagon—the very symbol of our military power—withstood great damage at the hands of extremists.

How do we respond to such an experience? Do we allow the Spirit of God to lead us into intercessory prayer that will produce change and determine whether we turn toward God or away from Him? Or do we allow the fear and the sorrow over this loss lead us into bitterness, anger, revenge and even greater defilements (see Heb. 12:15)? Do we cry out for mercy and grasp God's goodness in a way we have never grasped it

before? Or do we have the reaction that Job's wife had toward Job's sorrow and just say, "Curse God and die!" (Job 2:9).

JUDGMENT?

Was this a judgment on America? In an e-mail sent out shortly after the attacks, Dutch Sheets wrote:

> Great caution should be exercised in using the word "judgment" to *define* these events. Many Christians understand that America has been experiencing a degree of judgment for some time—sin has wages (see Rom. 6:23). But most biblical judgment is the inevitable, built-in consequence of sin, not the direct hand of God. He didn't pronounce curses after Adam and Eve's fall because He was an angry God who loves to curse sinners. He did so because of the inherent results of their actions. And He did it while covering their nakedness and promising redemption, a redemption involving great sacrificial love on His part—the incarnation and death of His Son (see Gen. 3:15). Also, rather than the direct hand of God, judgments are often simply the result of forfeiting God's favor and protection. Jonah 2:8 tells us: "Those who cling to worthless idols forfeit the grace that could be theirs." A careful and compassionate explanation of reaping, or the consequences of sin and of turning from God, should be our definition of the events. I would advise not even using the term "judgment" because the world will proba-bly not hear anything else we say.[1]

Rick Ridings, writing from Israel, sent the following inter-pretation of this event:

I believe the Scriptures show that such events are not specific judgment upon the individuals who happened to be in harm's way at that time. However, that does not take away from the fact that they can be judgment upon a nation and its idols. Jesus made this teaching clear in Luke 13:4,5: "Or those eighteen who died when the tower in Siloam fell on them—do you think they were more guilty than all the others living in Jerusalem? I tell you, no! But unless you repent, you too will all perish."

I believe judgment comes upon cities and nations when the accumulation of our sins finally forces a patient God to remove from us His gracious hand of protection, so that we get what we deserved all along. This principle is seen clearly, for example, in Isaiah 5:5: "Now I will tell you what I am going to do to my vineyard: I will take away its hedge, and it will be destroyed; I will break down its wall, and it will be trampled. I will make it a wasteland, neither pruned nor cultivated, and briers and thorns will grow there. I will command the clouds not to rain on it. The vineyard of the LORD Almighty is the house of Israel, and the men of Judah are the garden of his delight. And he looked for justice, but saw bloodshed; for righteousness, but heard cries of distress."

Totally aside from the question of whether this was some form of national judgment is the question of present judgment and the shaking of demonic powers. I believe God is saying that judgment has begun on the twin pillars of the worship of Mammon and the worship of Allah. These two systems of false worship hold much of the world back from true worship to the true God, the God of Abraham, Isaac, and Jacob, and His only begotten Son and our Savior and Lord, Jesus Christ (Yeshua ha Mashiach).[2]

THE WAR CONTINUES WITH A STRATEGY

A strategy is a set of plans that help us accomplish what we are being asked to accomplish. The Spirit of God will give us strategy in the midst of war so that we win! In *Releasing the Prophetic Destiny of a Nation*, I relate the following story:

> At the end of 2002 when I was flying into Washington, D.C. for meetings, the Lord impressed me with these words, *"For this nation to change, I need you to visit every state and rally My army."* This was a very stretching moment for my life. I speak and travel all over the world. I have a large family, a vibrant church, and serve on many ministry boards. Therefore, I knew that the Lord would have to fully confirm His word to me. He began by doing some very peculiar things to let me know He was working to assign me my next "gap" to stand in. Dutch Sheets met me in D.C. where we were having leadership gatherings and ministering, and asked me this question: "What do you hear the Lord saying?" I could only respond with the above—that He was asking me to go to every state of our nation. With a very peculiar look on his face, he said, "The Lord has spoken the same thing to me!" Thus, our lives would change the next two years with the promise that if we would *go*, the nation that we loved would also change.[3]

Another reason that I believe going from state to state materialized is because of the word that God gave me in October 2000 before the presidential election. For years, I had met with apostles, prophets and intercessors in various states across the country. However, it was now time to go to war for our nation by going to each state. This was God's strategy.

GOD HAS A PROPHETIC ARMY

States have destinies. Our nation was created sovereignly. The United States Constitution says, "We the People of the United States, in Order to form a more perfect Union, establish Justice, insure domestic Tranquility, provide for the common defense, promote the general Welfare, and secure the Blessings of Liberty to ourselves and our Posterity, do ordain and establish this Constitution for the United States of America." In the Declaration of Independence, we find:

> We, therefore, the Representatives of the United States of America, in General Congress, Assembled, appealing to the Supreme Judge of the world for the rectitude of our intentions, do, in the Name, and by Authority of the good People of these Colonies, solemnly publish and declare, That these United Colonies are, and of Right ought to be Free and Independent States; that they are Absolved from all Allegiance to the British Crown, and that all political connection between them and the State of Great Britain, is and ought to be totally dissolved; and that as Free and Independent States, they have full Power to levy War, conclude Peace, contract Alliances, establish Commerce, and to do all other Acts and Things which Independent States may of right do. And for the support of this Declaration, with a firm reliance on the protection of divine Providence, we mutually pledge to each other our Lives, our Fortunes and our sacred Honor.

In *Releasing the Prophetic Destiny of a Nation*, Dutch and I state the following regarding how we should view the destiny of the states that we live in:

Therefore, we should view the destiny of our state as part of the whole of what God has planned for our nation. This is the same concept as a body. Also, we should look at the Body of Christ in each state. When we align the Body of Christ in our nation we find a peculiar people ready to do God's will from heaven in the land that we occupy here in the earth. We, the Body of Christ, should be the driving force to even maintain our Constitution and the Declaration of Independence. Any time a state deviates from God's plan and His sovereign order in this nation, the Body of Christ should rise up in that state and say let us return and be restored the Lord.[4]

Dutch and I knew that the 50 state tour gatherings would be a key to our nation restoring its breastplate of righteousness. The major goal of the state gatherings was to align the Body of Christ properly and to decree the Lord's redemptive plan for each state. This would stir up the faith in the Body of Christ in each state and cause those in the Body to take their stand on behalf of their land. In *Releasing the Prophetic Destiny of a Nation,* Dutch and I write the following regarding this process:

One key to the transformation of our nation is for God's order to be established in each state. When strategic intercessors are aligned with apostolic leaders, breakthrough begins. Intercessors carry the burden of God, prophetic people make key declarations and apostles set the decrees in motion. In other words, intercessors keep the heavens open, prophets begin to express God's heart, making key declarations into the atmosphere, and apostolic leaders pull upon that revelation or blueprint of heaven and bring it into an established form in the earth realm.

After we connected with apostolic leadership in a territory, many times we would begin addressing an issue that had stopped God's redemptive covenant plan. We would declare restoration! Usually reconciliation would follow. Then God would release His purpose. We also would obey the word of God and pray for the authorities in our nation. . . . Then the meeting in a supernatural way touched the whole world.[5]

The 50 state tour meetings created a dynamic in our nation that will be passed on to generations to come. Even though war continues to wage, there is remnant filled with victory—and that remnant is increasing.

GOD IS MOVING THE CHURCH FROM FELLOWSHIP TO ARMY

What is going on in America is not unique. When God says that we are in a time of war, this applies to His Body in every nation. Isaiah 56:6-7 says that there will be a joyous House of Prayer for all *ethnos* groups in the earth. We just need to develop a victory mentality in this war and be filled with joy!

Victory is a state of triumph. To be victorious in war, we must understand our God, ourselves and our enemy. So, who are we? What is "the Church"? In Matthew 16:16, Peter taps into who Jesus really is when he proclaims, "You are the Christ, the Son of the living God." The Lord responds by saying:

Blessed are you, Simon Bar-Jonah, for flesh and blood has not revealed this to you, but My Father who is in heaven. And I also say to you that you are Peter, and on this rock I will build My church, and the gates of Hades shall not prevail against it. And I will give you the keys of

the kingdom of heaven, and whatever you bind on earth will be bound in heaven, and whatever you loose on earth will be loosed in heaven (Matt. 16:17-19).

Therefore, the Lord is saying that through this confession of revelation, He will call out and gather a group that will express His purposes—even to the gates of hell. He will give these whom he has called out keys of authority to bind and loose on Earth. This will allow them to forbid and permit. They will forbid the purposes of Satan to continue to permit, and they will permit God's full diverse expression of Himself to be seen in the earth.

Many people often confuse the Church with the kingdom of God. These two entities are not the same. The Kingdom is the overall structure that the Church is attempting to express in the earth. The Church exists to see the Kingdom established and operating on Earth. The Church facilitates the Kingdom.

To be victorious in war, we must understand our God, ourselves and our enemy.

There is conflict in the earth realm between kingdoms. The kingdom of God and the kingdom of Satan are at war! The Church operates as the armed forces of God in that war. The Church is the governing, legislating and mediating force that God has ordained and aligned to accomplish His purposes in the earth.

In *The Worship Warrior*, John Dickson and I write, "Worship and war go together. But for war we must have an army. An army is a nation's personnel organized for battle."[6] The concept of the Church is one of power, legislation and corporate association. We in the Church are a decreeing and demonstrating power in the earth.

In everything that occurs, there is usually a process involved. Process is the course of something developing and eventually coming into its full operation. Process includes preparation, discipline, order, change, development and operational steps that bring us to a destination. We go through a process to reach our destiny, and that process usually includes restoration, reconciliation and some sort of release.

A Prayer Focus to Advance in Victory

We are entering into a season when we must take quick and forcible possession of the opportunities that are presented to us by the Lord. To "seize" means to "grasp with the mind, apprehend, take into custody, or capture." We are going into a war with human reasoning that resists the changes that are ahead. *We must bring all of our thoughts into captivity and be ready to quickly obey the mind of the Spirit.*

Visions from the Lord are important. In December 2004, I was ministering in California, and as I was teaching I saw a huge wave. I said, "Lord, what am I seeing?" The Lord answered, "Waves of change are beginning to mount. You have a choice—you can either ride these waves of change and harness their power or you can resist change this year and be overwhelmed by destruction and decay."

To "change" means to "turn, to put in place, to make another, to pass away, to be transformed, or to produce a disguise (one of Satan's tactics)." We are in a season where the Spirit of God is shifting our thought processes. We are about to go a way that we have not gone before, and this will create an abrupt turn in many of our lives. This turn is linked with a change in mind called repentance. Repentance is not a bad word, but a gift of grace from God that produces joy and change. *This is not a season of condemnation because of our past mistakes, but a season of revelation that*

will produce victory over the past and open up our future.

Change creates a physical repositioning at times. Change causes us to be positioned spiritually in our abiding place (see Ps. 91). Change causes us to let go of issues in our past that create an idolatrous death in our future. If we receive the wave of His Spirit, our discernment will increase and we will see Satan's disguise removed.

Moving from Victory to Victory over the Next 10 Months

Victory can mean either final and complete supremacy in battle or war, or a triumph in a specific military engagement. Victory can also mean success in any contest or struggle involving the defeat of an opponent or the overcoming of obstacles. It is now time to move past the obstacles that prevent us from succeeding in what God is asking us to do! I believe that what defeats us most is a spirit of defeat or failure. This spirit is typically linked to our generations or to some situation in which we did not excel. Satan seems to use these things to put a mantle of reproach on us and give us a mind of fear instead of power.

One of the defining moments in history occurred on December 26, 2004. A massive earthquake shook Southeast Asia, creating a tsunami that redefined the earth's rotation axis. I was reading through the Bible at that time and came across Genesis 8:5-6: "And the waters decreased continually until the tenth month. In the tenth month, on the first day of the month, the tops of the mountains were seen. So it came to pass, at the end of forty days, that Noah opened the window of the ark which he had made." As I read this passage, it illuminated and seemed to literally leap from the page. I then heard the Lord say, "I am preparing 10 months of victory for My people. If they will develop a mind for victory, they will go from victory to victory.

Just as the waters decreased that had overcome the earth, I will cause the waters that have been attempting to overcome My people to decrease. They will find themselves standing on solid ground with clear vision. Set your eyes on the top of the mountain and watch your vision develop over the 10 months."

Many times, it takes praying and believing and decreeing with our mouth before our brain and all of its thought processes will shift. The following are some decrees and victory points that I wrote to help people develop a mind-set for victory in the year 2005 so that they may walk in triumph. Do not let the enemy push you back. Do not let your head be overtaken by the waters of circum-

Catch the waves of change and let them carry you into a whole new place— physically as well as spiritually.

stance around you. Catch the waves of change and let them carry you into a whole new place—physically as well as spiritually.

Victory Month 1. This is a time of sanctification. Set yourself apart and develop a mind for victory. Break the power of besetting sins and come into a new order. Beware of the enemy's strategy to block you. I see the enemy devising a plan at the gate to stop your entry way, *but God* is preparing your victory. This is a time to allow the Spirit to reorder your vision.

Victory Month 2. This is a month to seed. What you tithe will blossom. There is a grace for your offerings to multiply thirty-, sixty- and a hundredfold. This is a month to gain victory through giving and break the curse of robbing God. What you seed in the second month will begin to produce great fruit. Break a three year cycle of debt and declare that your past financial defeats will reverse and begin to multiply sevenfold.

Victory Month 3. This is a major month of change, and it will also be a month of travail. However, travail with joy, to bring forth. Declare a reversal over visions that were aborted. Set aside a Purim time in your life and celebrate, for the power of celebration will break through all barriers.

Victory Month 4. This is a month of breaking old cycles. Ask God for signs, wonders and miracles that will intervene in the old cyclical structures in your life. Make a list of old cycles that you need to break. If you praised last month, you can be secure in God's perfect timing this month. Declare that everything in your past be repaired and restored so that your future can be unlocked. This is a month in which you will gain victory in strategic warfare. Do not be afraid of ascending in worship. Find times to fast during this month. Look up and see the window of heaven that is opening over you. Ask God to open your eyes so that you can experience His glory.

Victory Month 5. You will be presented with a "Mt. Sinai" journey this month. Do not go around Mt. Sinai again, but begin to shout that you are going up to Zion! Ask for the Spirit of revelation and wisdom, and God will pour this upon you through the window of heaven. This is a month to war against legalistic structures. Declare a shift in the laws that Satan has illegally positioned. We must shift certain laws during this time frame so that they do not create a greater bondage over the next 40 years in this nation. Ask the Lord to take the lid off of evangelical structures and declare a great move of revival.

Victory Month 6. This is a month to leave old structures behind. It is easy to fall into idolatry or enter into an agreement with something in your past that could lead to idolatry, so find your new place of worship and decree that you will have victory over idolatry. This is a month to really analyze your connections and covering. Be sure you are submitting properly, for idolatry can create a setback in your inheritance (Numbers 14 will be a key passage to understand).

This is a month to overcome anger. Cut old past losses that are linked with bitterness and move on. Be absorbed in praise. A new level of supply will begin to be unlocked this month, so watch for new provisional strategies in the earth realm.

Victory Month 7. This is the month to gain victory over your thought processes. Allow the Lord to draw out old desires— He will remove some of these old desires and will activate others. Your thought life can be completely revolutionized during this time. However, this could also be your hardest month of war, so stick close to the Lord and develop a prayer shield around you.

This is a month for a new level of discernment to be released. Stay in the Word, pray in the spirit and allow the Lord to uncover some key issues related to the blood of Jesus, the glory of God and physical healing. If you celebrate this month, you will break through the "blood barrier" of old thought processes, which will produce a victory mentality for the rest of the year. Death strategies and assignments will break. You can have victory and experience healing of your mind this month. You can break double-mindedness and no longer have to be hung up between two opinions.

Victory Month 8. This is a month to seek the King. Do not be afraid to bring faults, failures and everything else about yourself into the Throne Room. Be ready to push forward quickly through intersections. Memorize Psalms 121 and 127. The Lord will make Himself available in night seasons through dreams and visions. He will be very near to those who seek Him while He is near. Expect abundant grace and mercy to be poured out upon you. Changes will culminate!

Victory Month 9. This is a month of reaping what you have sown. Those who have remained strong and faithful can expect to prosper in a new way. Receive a new measure of strength and ask God for mercy and grace. This is a month in which our words will become very important.

Victory Month 10. This is the month in which your testimony shall overcome the enemy's plan. Watch for victorious testimonies to break forth in the Body of Christ. The enemy will raise a standard against our testimony, *but God* will come in like a flood. Faith will explode and create an atmosphere in which things that could not happen will happen.

Stop! Prophetically shout, *"Victory!"* 10 times. Embrace all the change that God brings into your life and go from victory to victory. Here are some prayer points to help you focus in days ahead:

• Pray for God's power to be displayed in the earth realm. We are entering into a time of *transition of power.* Decree that the Church will demonstrate the power of God in each nation of the earth.
• Pray for the *restoration of the war mantle* to the Body of Christ. One of the greatest hindrances of prophetic fulfillment is to grow passive and stale in a time of war.
• Pray for a *supernatural repositioning* of the Body. This will allow those in the Body to stand in their proper boundaries and spheres of authority and wield the sword of the Spirit.
• Pray for a *supernatural linking and binding between the generations.* When three generations are agreeing and decreeing the word of the Lord, the Glory of God restores a release in the earth (see Isa. 59—60).
• Pray that *the plowman shall overtake the reaper.* This will move us from one dimension of harvest to another dimension of harvest. Amos 9 (especially verse 13) is a key passage.
• Pray that *teams of plowmen will be connected together.* No one is strong enough to plow alone. This is a time for apos-

tolic, prophetic teams to rise up throughout the world.

• Pray that *humility* abounds in the Body of Christ. *There will be many "humility meetings" in days ahead.* These meetings will provide opportunities to restore covenants that the enemy has attempted to break in the past.

• Pray that *the Church will continue to increase in mercy toward the Jews.* This will cause the world to resist the Church. Watch for this to occur in cities with large Jewish populations, such as New York City, Miami-West Palm Beach, Los Angeles, Detroit, Houston, Dallas, Buenos Aires, Paris, Moscow and Madrid). In addition, ministry to other ethnicities will also increase. Look for the wall of ethnicity to break down. The Church has not fully understood covenant, but this will produce a restoration of God's covenant in the earth realm.

• Pray for *apostles, prophets, pastors and teachers to make room for the evangelist that is arising in this hour.* Expect God to do a new thing in the earth when the Church is properly aligned. Once God's government is in place, the world's governments will begin to shake. He will redo pastoral thinking and cause the shepherds to be hungry for the glory of God.

• *Pray for confidence.* Confidence results in boldness, which results in awakening. *The ability to produce the next move of God is within you.* Do not keep looking at the past patterns of revival, but recognize that the next move of God is already within you. This is a new move of God like nothing we've ever seen before.

Is the Best Yet Ahead?

Lawlessness, terrorism and anti-Semitism are three forces that are rising in the earth realm.[7] We are seeing a war over God's

covenant with the earth. Psalm 24:1 states, "The earth is the Lord's, and all its fullness," and the enemy knows that the Lord's fullness of purpose will be done in the earth realm. Therefore, there is a visible war raging that is backed by Satan's kingdom. This war is to stop the fullness of God's purpose manifesting in His people.

With this war now visibly raging, *is the best yet ahead?* With fundamental Islam becoming a global threat that is vying for the conversion and allegiance of souls in the earth, *is the best yet ahead?* With hate groups increasing and hate breeding hate, *is the best yet ahead?* With the spirit of lawlessness manifesting in the next generation, *is the best yet ahead?* With wars and rumors of wars, *is the best yet ahead?* Psalm 20 is a wonderful confession to make:

> May the LORD answer you in the day of trouble;
> May the name of the God of Jacob defend you;
> May He send you help from the sanctuary,
> And strengthen you out of Zion;
> May He remember all your offerings,
> And accept your burnt sacrifice. Selah.
>
> May He grant you according to your heart's desire,
> And fulfill all your purpose.
> We will rejoice in your salvation,
> And in the name of our God we will set up our banners!
> May the LORD fulfill all your petitions.
>
> Now I know that the LORD saves His anointed;
> He will answer him from His holy heaven
> With the saving strength of His right hand.
>
> Some trust in chariots, and some in horses;
> But we will remember the name of the LORD our God.

They have bowed down and fallen;
But we have risen and stand upright.

Save, LORD!
May the King answer us when we call.

Is the best ahead? *Yes, if His people who are called by His name will humble themselves and seek His face!*

A PROPHECY AND CALL TO ADVANCE!

God is saying to us, "This is a new day! Plant your feet and determine not to go backward. The enemy will assault you to press you backward. Have I not said, 'Without a prophetic vision the people perish and go backward?' I am ready to revisit areas that have advanced My purposes but that retreated at the day of battle. This is the beginning of the shaking of governments. There must be a confrontation of governments. My government on Earth is arising and causing entire regions to shake. I am restoring and raising up leaders. I am causing My governments and My gifts to align. This is creating great shakings from region to region throughout this land. This alignment is creating a shift in civil government.

"Today is a day of breaking off that which caused My church to retreat from the visitations of the past. Many advanced and then retreated—*now* is a time to advance! There will be great connections occurring in My Body in this advance. This will be the beginning of confronting sorcery, astrology and witchcraft, which have produced control. I am sending you forth and releasing supernatural wisdom. This wisdom will dethrone the sorcerers, astrologers and practitioners of witchcraft throughout regions.

"Love and confidence is arising in My Body. From worship, you will now move into a new supernatural dimension. Do not

fear this call to the supernatural. The Pharaoh systems of this nation will begin to strengthen to keep My kingdom paradigms from forming and advancing in the earth! Do not fear these systems, but keep confronting through prayer the powers that have attached themselves to the structures of governments in your region. I will make you into a supernatural people who can rise up and overthrow that which has controlled you in the past and will control you in the future. My people are becoming a new, sharp threshing instrument. This threshing is producing shaking. This shaking is releasing Harvest. This is the beginning of a consuming fire. Fire must be in your heart. The fear of the supernatural is to be removed from you. Religious spirits and occultism have produced fear over the supernatural spirits. Therefore, they have retreated in their prayer life and fallen into passivity.

"This is the beginning of a new day. Plant your feet. The window of opportunity for change is short. This will be a time that night watches are re-formed in your region, and I will revisit you in the night watch. I will visit my Bride as I described in Song of Solomon and knock upon her door. This is not a time for hesitation. Night watches will spring forth across this land. Once again these watches will open the door to Me, and I will come again. Therefore, I am calling watchmen to arise and cry out day and night for my Bride to be positioned near the door of opportunity in the nations of the earth. Be positioned, ready to open the door of opportunity in your nation. My Bride must not hesitate to open the door. Harvest is waiting to come through the door into the storehouse of My kingdom.

"My will has been activated on Earth. I am advancing. Advance with Me, and I will lead you into warfare. Many have grown fearful of confronting the enemy. I came to destroy the works of the enemy. I confronted both legalism and liberalism. I say rise up in worship that you might confront. Without confrontation, your enemy, the legalist, will gain much strength

against you and narrow the boundaries of your freedom. If you will align yourselves properly and allow your gift to work within My government, I will guide you like a troop into warfare and make you victorious. Worship is arising. From worship, you will war! For a sound of war is coming into the heart of My people. Do not go backward. Take off the old garments that would hinder you. My *advance* is now in the earth.

"You have been blinded from the supply of the future. A new seer anointing is about to arise in My people. What you couldn't see in the past, you will now see. You've tried to connect and align with some, but now I will release a new anointing for connecting. You will see strategies of supply that have been hidden from you by occult powers. The seer anointing is coming back into your region. My people's eyes are about to see their supply. Advance is now in the earth. Open your eyes and advance with Me. You will know Me as Jehovah Jireh! You will know Me as Jehovah Nissi! I, Lord *Sabaoth*, will now begin to release a manifestation from region to region throughout this land! Let Me clothe you with *favor* and *authority*! Advance!"

Notes

1. Dutch Sheets, "A Biblical Response to the Terrorist Attacks on America for the purpose of Prayer and Evangelism," September 13, 2001. Used by permission.
2. Rick Ridings in Jerusalem, "How Should We Pray in the Aftermath of September 11th?" October 19, 2001. Used by permission.
3. Dutch Sheets and Chuck D. Pierce, *Releasing the Prophetic Destiny of a Nation* (Shippensburg, PA: Destiny Image, 2005), p. 28.
4. Ibid., p. 45. For examples of how the Lord released the destiny of states, refer to chapter 8, "State by State: A History and Future Destiny."
5. Ibid., pp. 45-46.
6. Chuck D. Pierce with John Dickson, *The Worship Warrior* (Ventura, CA: Regal Books, 2002), p. 243.
7. For more on this topic of lawlessness, terrorism and anti-Semitism, see Chuck Pierce and Rebecca Sytsema, *The Future War of the Church* (Ventura, CA: Regal Books, 2001).

Scripture Index

Subject Index

OTHER BOOKS BY CHUCK D. PIERCE AND REBECCA WAGNER SYTSEMA

The Future War of the Church
How We Can Defeat Lawlessness and Bring God's Order to the Earth

Possessing Your Inheritance
Moving Forward in God's Covenant Plan for Your Life

Prayers That Outwit the Enemy
Making God's Word Your First Line of Defense

Protecting Your Home from Spiritual Darkness
How We Can Defeat Lawlessness and Bring God's Order to the Earth

When God Speaks
How to Interpret Dreams, Visions, Signs and Wonders